我的亲情美文
让我陪你慢慢变老

英汉对照　词汇解析　语法讲解　励志语录

马琼琼　编著

中国纺织出版社有限公司

图书在版编目（CIP）数据

我的亲情美文：让我陪你慢慢变老：英文／马琼琼编著. -- 北京：中国纺织出版社有限公司，2019.12
ISBN 978-7-5180-6371-0

Ⅰ.①我… Ⅱ.①马… Ⅲ.①英语—语言读物 Ⅳ.①H319.4

中国版本图书馆CIP数据核字（2019）第138339号

策划编辑：武洋洋　　责任校对：韩雪丽
责任设计：晏子茹　　责任印制：储志伟

中国纺织出版社有限公司出版发行
地址：北京市朝阳区百子湾东里A407号楼　邮政编码：100124
销售电话：010-67004422　传真：010-87155801
http://www.c-textilep.com
中国纺织出版社天猫旗舰店
官方微博http://www.weibo.com/2119887771
三河市延风印装有限公司印刷　各地新华书店经销
2019年12月第1版第1次印刷
开本：880×1230　1/32　印张：6.25
字数：200千字　定价：39.80元

凡购本书，如有缺页、倒页、脱页，由本社图书营销中心调换

前言

思想结晶改变人生命运，经典美文提高生活品位。曾几何时，一个字，触动你的心弦；一句话，让你泪流满面；一篇短文，让你重拾信心，勇敢面对生活给你的考验。这就是语言的魅力。通过阅读优美的英文短文，不仅能够扩大词汇量，掌握单词的用法，了解语法，学习地道的表达，更让你的心灵如沐春风，得到爱的呵护和情感的滋养。

岁月流转，经典永存。针对英语学习爱好者的需要，编者精心选取了难易适中的英语经典美文，为你提供一场丰富多彩的文学盛宴。本书采用中英文对照的形式，便于读者理解。每篇美文后都附有单词解析、语法知识点、经典名句三大版块，让你在欣赏完一篇美文后，还能扩充词汇量、巩固语法知识、斟酌文中好句，并感悟人生。在一篇篇不同题材风格的英语美文中，你总能找到引起你心灵共鸣的一篇。

读一本新书恰似坠入爱河，是场冒险。你得全身心地投入进去。翻开书页之时，从前言直至封底你或许都知之甚少。但谁又不是呢？字里行间的只言片语不总是正确的。

有时候你会发现，人们自我推销时是一种形象，等你在深入了解后，他们就完全变样了。有时故事的叙述流于表面，朴实的语言，平淡的情节，但阅读过半后，你却发觉这本书真是出乎意料的妙不可言，而这种感受只能靠自己去感悟！

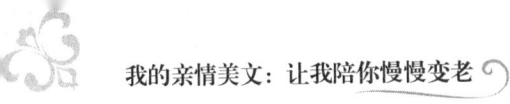

阅读之乐，腹有诗书气自华；阅读之美，活水云影共天光。阅读可以放逐百年孤独，阅读可以触摸千年月光。阅读中有眼前的收获，阅读中也有诗和远方。

让我们静下心来感受英语美文的温度，在英语美文中仔细品味似曾相识的细腻情感，感悟生命和人性的力量。

编者
2019年9月

目录

01 Remember We Are Raising Children, Not Flowers
　　牢记，我们是养育孩子，不是养花 001

02 The Mother with One Eye
　　只有一只眼睛的母亲 007

03 A Gift of Love
　　爱的礼物 013

04 Love Is a Two-way Street
　　爱，是一条双行道 019

05 Fatal Suspicion
　　致命的怀疑 024

06 Mom Is Child's Angel
　　妈妈是孩子的守护天使 029

07 A Letter to Dear Dad on Father's Day
　　父亲节之日写给父亲的一封信 034

08 Never Give Up On the People You Love
　　绝不要放弃你所爱的人 039

09 A Father's Love
　　父爱 044

10 A Father and a Son
　　父子俩 049

11 Promise
　　永恒的承诺 055

12 A Special Letter
　　一封特殊的信 061

I

13 Mom, I Got My Attitude from You, and That's Not a Bad Thing!
妈妈，这倔劲儿随你，而这不是一件坏事！..................066

14 Mother's Hands
妈妈的双手..071

15 A Letter from Mom to Two Daughters
一位母亲写给女儿的信..076

16 Seven Ways to Show Your Love to Your Father
七种方式向父亲表达你的爱..082

17 Some Wounds from Mother
来自母亲的疤痕..088

18 What Do Parents Owe Their Children?
父母到底欠子女什么？..094

19 Run Through the Rain
雨中的记忆..099

20 Not a Simple Dress
不凡的连衣裙..104

21 The Key of a Car
一把车钥匙..109

22 A Box Full of Kisses
装满吻的盒子..115

23 Not Just a Mom
母亲的含义..120

24 All You Remember
你所记得的一切..125

25 Brother's Wish
哥哥的心愿..131

26 The Apple Tree
苹果树..136

27 New Shoes
一双新鞋子..141

Contents 目录

28 I Will Always Forgive You
我会永远原谅你 147

29 Stand Tall
站直了 152

30 The Games Sisters Play
那些属于我们姐妹的游戏 157

31 The Meanest Mother
无情的母亲 162

32 Just What My Father Always Wanted
总能让爸爸高兴的礼物 167

33 The Memorable Cooler
冷藏箱里的难忘回忆 172

34 Your Name in Gold
金制你的名字 178

35 Papa's New Pants
爸爸的新裤子 183

01 Remember We Are Raising Children, Not Flowers
牢记，我们是养育孩子，不是养花

I recently heard a story from Stephen Glenn about a famous research scientist who had made several very important medical **breakthroughs**. He was being interviewed by a newspaper reporter who asked him why he thought he was able to be so much more creative than the average person. What set him so far apart from others?

He responded that, in his opinion, it all came from an experience with his mother that occurred when he was about two years old. He had been trying to remove a bottle of milk from the refrigerator when he lost his grip on the **slippery** bottle and it fell, spilling its contents all over the kitchen floor—a **veritable** sea of milk!

When his mother came into the kitchen, instead of yelling at him, giving him a **lecture** or punishing him, she said, "Robert, what a great and wonderful mess you have made! I have rarely seen such a huge puddle of milk. Well, the damage has already been done. Would you like to get down and play in the milk for a few minutes before we

我最近从斯蒂芬·格伦那里听到一位有着几项重大医疗领域上突破的科学研究者的故事。新闻记者曾采访过他，问他为什么比一般人更具有创造力？究竟是什么潜在因素让他如此卓尔不凡？

他说，在他看来，这一切都应与他两岁左右时母亲对发生在他身上的事有关。当时他试着挪动一瓶冰箱里面的牛奶，一不小心，没有拿稳，于是瓶子从手中滑落然后掉在了地上，牛奶溅的满地都是——看上去宛如茫茫乳海！

母亲闻声赶紧走进厨房，可并没有对他大喊大叫，也没有狠狠地教训或者惩罚他，只是说："小罗伯特，你这个小家伙，看看你给我带来的小小意外！我可从不曾见过这么大片的牛奶坑。好吧，你坏事都做完了，待你把这收拾好前，你能先停会再玩吗？"

然后，他这么做了。几分钟后，母亲说道："说真的，小罗伯特，无论你什么时候给我

clean it up?"

Indeed, he did. After a few minutes, his mother said, "You know, Robert, whenever you make a mess like this, **eventually** you have to clean it up and **restore** everything to its proper order. So, how would you like to do that? We could use a sponge, a towel or a mop. Which do you prefer?" He chose the **sponge** and together they cleaned up the spilled milk.

His mother then said, "You know, what we have here is a failed experiment in how to effectively cry a big milk bottle with two tiny hands. Let's go out in the back yard and fill the bottle with water and see if you can discover a way to carry it without dropping it." The little boy learned that if he grasped the bottle at the top near the lip with both hands, he could carry it without dropping it. What a wonderful lesson!

This **renowned** scientist then remarked that it was at that moment that he knew he didn't need to be afraid to make mistakes. Instead, he learned that mistakes were just opportunities for learning something new, which is, after all, what scientific experiments are all about. even if the experiment "doesn't work," We usually learn something **valuable** from it.

Wouldn't it be great if all parents

们制造了点意外，到最后你都不得不自己收拾烂摊子然后把所有东西放回到原位。所以，接下来你打算怎么办呢？我们可以选择的有——海绵抹布，用毛巾或者是拖布，你觉得哪个好呢？"我挑了海面抹布然后和妈妈一起把满地打翻的牛奶收拾干净了。

母亲接着又说："你瞧，在这里我们试着怎样有成效地用双小手拿着大瓶子的实验失败了。我们去后院吧，在那把瓶子装满水，然后看看我们能不能找到不让瓶子撒出水来的方法？"这个小家伙——也就是我，学到了当双手握紧瓶子口附近的地方时，瓶子才不会被打翻。多么有趣的发现！

这位赫赫有名的科学家后来谈到，也就是在那个时候他明白了无须恐惧去犯下错误。相反地，错误往往是学习新知识的良机，科学试验又何尝不是呢？即使试验失败了，我们还是可以从中学到很多有价值的东西。

如果所有的父母都能像小罗伯特母亲那样善于应对孩子们所犯的小错误，那就太好了。

Remember We Are Raising Children, Not Flowers
牢记，我们是养育孩子，不是养花

would respond the way Robert's mother responded to him?

单词解析 Word Analysis

breakthrough [b'reɪkθruːz] *n.* 突破点，重要的新发现

例 The company looks poised to make a significant breakthrough in China.
这家公司看来很有把握在中国取得重大突破。

slippery ['slɪpəri] *adj.* 滑的；滑头的

例 Motorists were warned to beware of slippery conditions.
提醒驾车人要当心路滑。

veritable ['verɪtəbl] *adj.* 名副其实的；真正的

例 We hate and loathe these veritable fiends.
我们痛恨和厌恶这些不折不扣的魔鬼。

lecture ['lektʃə(r)] *n.* 教训，训斥

例 Our captain gave us a stern lecture on safety.
船长就安全问题严厉地训斥了我们一顿。

eventually [ɪ'ventʃuəli] *adv.* 最后，终于

例 She sees the bar as a starting point and eventually plans to run her own chain of country inns.
她把那间酒吧当作一个起点，最终计划是经营自己的乡村旅馆连锁店。

sponge [spʌndʒ] *n.* 海绵，海绵状物

例 He wiped off the table with a sponge.
他用一块海绵擦桌子。

renowned [rɪ'naʊnd] *adj.* 有名的，有声望的

例 It is renowned as one of the region's best restaurants.
这是本地区最好的饭店之一。

valuable ['væljuəbl] *adj.* 贵重的，宝贵的，有价值的

例 The golden rule is never to clean a valuable coin.
重要的原则是决不清除贵重硬币上的污垢。

语法知识点 *Grammar Points*

① What set him so far apart from others?

set apart from 区别；把……区分开

例 Her clear and elegant prose sets her apart from most other journalists.
她的散文凝练高雅，多数新闻工作者无出其右。

What sets it apart from hundreds of similar small French towns is the huge factory.
与其他数百个法国小镇不同的是它拥有巨大的工厂。

set apart 留出；分开放；隔离开；突出

例 One day of the week should be set apart for relaxation.
每周应该拨出一天时间休闲。

类似的词组：set about 开始；散布（谣言等）；开始，着手 set aside 提出；把……置于一旁 set against 使敌视，使对立

② Robert, what a great and wonderful mess you have made!

以上是what引导的感叹句，用来表示人的强烈感情。一般说来，what引导的感叹句有三种句式，此时，what为形容词，用作定语，修饰它后面的名词或名词词组。具体如下：

1. What a/an+形容词+可数名词单数+主语+谓语！

例 What a nice day it is!
多么好的天气啊！

2. What+形容词+可数名词复数形式+主语+谓语！

例 What good teachers they are!
他们是多么好的老师啊！

3. What+形容词+不可数名词+主语+谓语！

例 What delicious food it is!
这是多么美味的食物啊！

Remember We Are Raising Children, Not Flowers
牢记，我们是养育孩子，不是养花

make a mess 弄得乱七八糟

例 He made a mess of his work.
他把工作搞得乱七八糟。

③ Let's go out in the back yard and fill the bottle with water and see if you can discover a way to carry it without dropping it.

fill...with 把……装满

例 The Dutch developed a custom by which children put out shoes which Saint Nicholas would fill with gifts when he came visiting.
荷兰人有一套自己的风俗，孩子们会将鞋子放在外面，圣诞老人到来时便会在里面装满礼品。

Jack filled his pockets with chestnuts.
杰克将口袋装满栗子。

fill...with=be filled with, be filled with系表结构在英语中经常用到。

例 The young man is filled with joy.
那个青年内心充满喜悦。

The soldiers were filled with anger.
战士们满腔怒火。

经典名句 Famous Classics

1. A mother is not a person to lean on but a person to make leaning unnecessary.
   母亲不是赖以依靠的人，而是使依靠成为不必要的人。

2. All I am, or can be, I owe to my angel mother.
   我之所有，我之所能，都归功于我天使般的母亲。

3. If the whole world betrayed you, at least your mother will not give up. Still remember childhood mother's embrace is the most beautiful paradise.
   如果整个世界都抛弃了你，至少还有母亲不会放弃你。还记得儿时母亲的怀抱就是我最美的天堂。

4. God cannot be everywhere. So God created Mom.
   上帝不能无处不在，所以他创造了"妈妈"。

5. All happy families are like one another; each unhappy family is unhappy in its own way.
所有幸福的家庭都十分相似，而每个不幸的家庭各有各自的不幸。

读书笔记

02 The Mother with One Eye
只有一只眼睛的母亲

My mother had only one eye. When I was growing up, I hated her for it. I hated the **uninvited** attention it got me at school. I hated how the other children stared at her and looked away in disgust. My mother worked two jobs to provide for the family, but I was just **embarrassed** by her and didn't want to be seen with her.

As I grew up, I did whatever was in my power to **distance** myself from my mother. I studied hard and got a job overseas so I wouldn't have to meet her. I got married and started raising a family of my own. I got busy with my job and family and with providing a comfortable life for my beloved children. I didn't even think about my mother anymore.

Out of the blue, my mother came to visit one day. Her one-eyed face scared my young children and they started crying. I was angry at my mother for showing up **unannounced** and I forbid her to ever return to my home and new family life. I yelled and screamed, but my mother quietly apologized and left without saying another word.

An invitation to a high school

我妈妈只有一只眼睛。在我成长的过程中，我非常讨厌这样的她。我讨厌在学校受到的不请自来的关注的眼神。我讨厌别的孩子盯着她然后厌恶地转过头去。为了支撑这个家，我妈妈要做两份工作，但我却只觉得她令我很尴尬，不想被看到和她在一起。

随着我慢慢长大，我一直尽一切所能远离我的母亲。为了出国工作我努力学习，这样就可以再也不见到她。我结了婚，建立了自己的家庭。我忙于工作、家庭，为我爱的孩子提供舒适的生活。我甚至不再去想我的妈妈了。

突然有一天，妈妈来看我。她的一只眼睛吓哭了我年幼的孩子。对于我母亲的突然造访我非常生气，我要求她永远不要来我家，不要接触我现在的家庭生活。我尖声叫喊着，但是母亲安静地道了歉，没有再多说一句话就离开了。

几十年后，受高中聚会的邀请，我回到了我的故乡。我忍不住开车路过儿时的家，在

reunion took me back to my hometown after decades. I could not resist driving past my childhood home and stopping by the old shack. My neighbors told me my mother had passed away and left a letter for me.

"My dear child:

I must begin by apologizing for visiting your home unannounced and frightening your beautiful children. I am also deeply sorry that I was such an embarrassment and source of **humiliation** to you when you were growing up.

I have learned that you may be coming back to town for your reunion. I may no longer be there when you come, and I think it is time to tell you an incident that happened when you were a young child. You see, my dear child, you were involved in an accident and lost one eye. I was **devastated** at the thought of my beloved child growing up with only one eye. I wanted you to see the beautiful world in all its **glory**, so I gave you my eye.

My dear child, I always have and always will love you from the bottom of my heart. I have never **regretted** my decision to give you my eye, and I am at peace that I was able to give you the ability to enjoy a complete life.

Your loving mother."

一幢老屋门口停了下来。邻居们告诉我，母亲已经去世了，留下了一封信给我。

"我亲爱的孩子：

在开头我必须为突然出现在你家并吓坏了你可爱的孩子们而道歉。在你成长过程中我是如此令你尴尬，让你受辱，对此我也深深地自责。

我得知你会在聚会的时候回来，但那时候我可能已经不在了，我想是时候该告诉你，在你小时候发生过一场意外。你知道的，我亲爱的孩子，你在那场事故中失去了一只眼睛。我无法接受和想象自己亲爱的孩子只能拥有一只眼睛。我想让你骄傲地看看这个美丽的世界，所以我把我的眼睛给了你。

我亲爱的孩子，我真心爱你，无论从前还是未来。我从没后悔把眼睛给了你，让你能够享受完整的生命，我死而无憾。

爱你的妈妈。"

The Mother with One Eye 只有一只眼睛的母亲 02

单词解析 Word Analysis

uninvited [ˌʌnɪnˈvaɪtɪd] *adj.* 未经要求的，未获邀请的，不速而至的

例 She tactfully discouraged their uninvited guests from staying longer.
她巧妙地使这些不请自到的客人知趣儿，没有再待下去。

embarrassed [ɪmˈbærəst] *adj.* 窘迫的；惭愧的；尴尬的

例 Polly, bewildered and embarrassed, dropped her head and scuffed her feet.
波莉既困惑又尴尬，低下头拖着脚走开了。

distance [ˈdɪstəns] *v.* 把……远远甩在后面；疏远；与……保持距离

例 The author distanced himself from some of the comments in his book.
作者使自己书中的某些评论不带个人色彩。

unannounced [ˌʌnəˈnaʊnst] *adj.* 名副其实的；真正的

例 My first night in Saigon I paid an unannounced visit to my father's cousins.
到西贡的第一个晚上，我给父亲的堂兄堂弟们来了个突然袭击。

reunion [riːˈjuːniən] *n.* （家庭、学校及其他团体成员的）团聚，重聚，聚会

例 The whole family was there for this big family reunion.
全家人都来参加了这次盛大的家庭聚会。

humiliation [hjuːˌmɪlɪˈeɪʃn] *n.* 耻辱；屈辱；丢脸；蒙羞

例 She faced the humiliation of discussing her husband's affair.
她面临了要谈及丈夫外遇的羞辱。

devastated [ˈdevəsteɪtɪd] *adj.* 极为震惊难过的；非常伤心的

例 Teresa was devastated; her dreams shattered.
特雷莎伤心欲绝——她的梦想彻底破灭了。

glory ['glɔːri] *n.* 光荣；荣耀

例 We were still basking in the glory of our Championship win.
我们依然沉浸在夺得锦标赛冠军的荣耀中。

regret [rɪɡˈret] *v.* 对……感到后悔，因……遗憾

例 I simply gave in to him, and I've regretted it ever since.
我就向他屈服了，从那以后我一直后悔。

语法知识点 *Grammar Points*

① I got married and started raising a family of my own. I got busy with my job and family and with providing a comfortable life for my beloved children.

get married 结婚，也可用be married，这里的marry作为不及物动词。

例 My best friend got married last weekend.
我最好的朋友上个周末结婚了。

get married/be married这两个短语后又都可接介词to+sb，表示"和……结婚"，这里我们一般不用get married with，这是习惯用法，约定俗成。

例 She got/was married to a teacher.
她和一个老师结婚了。

② Out of the blue, my mother came to visit one day.

对于blue这个词，大家一定是再熟悉不过的。除了"蓝色"，还表示"忧伤"，我们熟悉的音乐类型蓝调，也是由此而来。out of blue这个短语应用最广泛的意思是"突然地，意外地"。

表示"突然"的单词或短语非常多，比如suddenly, abruptly, unexpectedly, all at once，all of a sudden等。

例 There are so many things out of the blue in our life.
生活中就是有这么多出乎意料的事情。

例 The job offer came out of the blue, and I had to make a choice immediately.
这个工作机会来得太突然，我必须马上做出选择。

The Mother with One Eye
只有一只眼睛的母亲

③ I could not resist driving past my childhood home and stopping by the old shack.

resist doing sth. 反对做某事，抵制做某事，忍住去做

例 And don't make the log complicated—that will only make you resist doing the log.
不要把日志做得很复杂——那样只会使你对做记录产生抵触情绪。

stop by /drop by 顺道拜访

例 Why not stop by his office by office hours?
为什么不在办公时间去他办公室里谈谈？

经典名句 Famous Classics

1. Placid parents make a placid home.
   平和的父母创造温馨的家。

2. Where we love is home, home that our feet may leave, but not our hearts.
   家是我们所爱的地方，双脚可以离开，心却不能。

3. From your parents you learn love and laughter and how to put one foot before the other.
   你从父母那里学到爱，学到笑，学到怎样走路。

4. A good mother is worth a hundred schoolmasters.
   一个好母亲相当于一百个好老师。

5. Be it ever so humble, there is no place like home.
   金窝，银窝，不如自家的草窝。

6. If you are a winter grass, affection is the sun, warming your cold body.
   如果你是冬日的小草，亲情就是太阳，为你温暖冰冷的身躯。

7. People always say that father's love is so quiet but grand that it seems like a mountain. They always bury their love to children deep in the bottom of their hearts and never show it.
   人们总说父爱如山，安静、伟岸，他们总把对孩子的爱深埋心底，从

不显露。

读书笔记

03 A Gift of Love
爱的礼物

"Can I see my baby?" The happy new mother asked.

When the **bundle** was nestled in her arms and she moved the fold of cloth to look upon his tiny face, she gasped. The doctor turned quickly and looked out the tall hospital window. The baby had been born without ears.

Time proved that the baby's hearing was perfect. It was only his appearance that was **marred**. When he rushed home from school one day and **flung** himself into his mother's arms, she sighed, knowing that his life was to be a succession of heartbreaks.

He blurted out the **tragedy**. "A boy, a big boy...called me a freak."

He grew up, handsome except for his **misfortune**. A favorite with his fellow students, he might have been class president, but for that. He developed a gift, a talent for literature and music.

"But you might mingle with other young people." His mother reproved him, but felt a kindness in her heart.

The boy's father had a session with the family physician... "Could nothing

"我可以看看我的宝宝吗？"初为人母的她开心地问道。

当裹着的婴儿放到她臂弯里，她掀开裹着婴儿的布，在看到他的小脸时，她不禁倒吸了一口气。医生快速地转过身，透过医院的高层窗户向外看去。婴儿生下来就没有耳朵。

时间证明婴儿的听力毫无问题，只是有损他的相貌。一天，当他匆匆从学校跑回家，扑向母亲的怀抱时，她叹了口气，意识到他的生活注定会受到一连串的打击。

他脱口诉说遭到的不幸："一个男孩，一个大个子男孩……他喊我怪胎。"

他长大了，虽然不幸但还是长得挺帅。颇受同学的欢迎，要不是有缺陷，他很可能当了班长。他对文学和音乐很有天赋和潜质。

"但你可能会和其他年轻人一样。"母亲责备地说，但从心底里觉得很欣慰。

男孩的父亲与家庭医生

013

be done?"

"I believe I could graft on a pair of outer ears, if they could be procured." The doctor decided. So the search began for a person who would make such a **sacrifice** for a young man.

Two years went by. Then, "You're going to the hospital, son. Mother and I have someone who will donate the ears you need. But it's a secret." said the father.

The operation was a brilliant success, and a new person emerged. His talents blossomed into genius, and school and college became a series of **triumphs**.

Later he married and entered the diplomatic service. "But I must know," he asked his father, "Who gave me the ears? Who gave me so much? I could never do enough for him."

"I do not believe you could," said the father, "but the agreement was that you are not to know...not yet."

The years kept their profound secret, but the day did come. One of the darkest days that ever pass through a son. He stood with his father over his mother's **casket**. Slowly, tenderly, the father stretched forth a hand and raised the thick, reddish brown hair to reveal that the mother had no outer ears.

"Mother said she was glad she

商量……"难道真无法补救吗？"

"我认为可以移植一双外耳，如果能够找到的话。"医生做了决定，于是他们开始寻求一个愿意为这个年轻人做出牺牲的人。

两年过去了。父亲对儿子说，"孩子，你要住院了。我和你妈找到愿意为你捐献耳朵的人了。但要求保密。"

手术获得了巨大成功，一个新人诞生了。他的潜力发展成一个天才，在中学和大学都取得了一连串的成功。

后来他结婚了，进入外交行业工作。一天，他问父亲："是谁给我的耳朵？谁给了我那么多？我做多少都无法报答他/她。"

"我也这样认为，"父亲说，"但是协议上说你不能知道……还不到时候。"

他们的秘密遵守了很多年，但这天终于来了，这也是儿子度过的最黑暗的日子。他和父亲站在母亲的棺材前，慢慢地、轻柔地，父亲向前伸出一只手，掀开母亲浓密的、红褐色的头发：母亲竟然没有耳朵！

"你母亲说过她很高兴，

never let her hair be cut," he whispered gently, "and nobody ever thought mother less beautiful, did they?"

她从不理发，"父亲轻柔地低声说，"但没人觉得母亲没以前美丽，是吧？"

单词解析 Word Analysis

bundle ['bʌndl] *n.* 婴儿；捆，束，包

例 You can refer to a tiny baby as a bundle.
可以把小婴儿称作"bundle"。
She produced a bundle of notes and proceeded to count out 195 pounds.
她拿出一捆钞票，接着数出了195英镑。

mar ['mɑ:] *v.* 毁坏，损坏，玷污

例 A number of problems marred the smooth running of this event.
许多问题影响了这件事的顺利进行。

fling [flɪŋ] *v.* 扔，猛扔

例 He once seized my knitting, flinging it across the room.
有一次他抓过我织的东西，把它扔到了屋子的另一头。

tragedy ['trædʒədi] *n.* 不幸；灾难；惨剧

例 They have suffered an enormous personal tragedy.
他们遭逢了巨大的个人不幸。

misfortune [ˌmɪsˈfɔ:tʃu:n] *n.* 不幸，灾祸

例 She seemed to enjoy the misfortunes of others.
她似乎喜欢幸灾乐祸。

sacrifice ['sækrɪfaɪs] *n.* 牺牲，舍弃，献出

例 Her husband's pride was a small thing to sacrifice for their children's security.
为了孩子们的安全，舍弃她丈夫的尊严不算什么。

triumphs ['traɪəmfs] *n.* 非凡的成功，杰出的成就
- 例 The championships proved to be a personal triumph for the coach.
事实证明，在这次锦标赛中教练取得了非凡的个人成就。

profound [prə'faʊnd] *adj.* 深刻的，强烈的，巨大的
- 例 This is a book full of profound, original and challenging insights.
这本书充满了深刻、新颖、令人深思的见解。

casket ['kɑːskɪt] *n.* 棺材；首饰盒
- 例 The pretty casket is given to her by her former boyfriend.
这个漂亮的首饰盒是她以前的男朋友送给她的。
The casket is in rosewood, brass and ivory marquetry.
棺材是紫檀木，黄铜和象牙镶嵌。

语法知识点 Grammar Points

① She sighed, knowing that his life was to be a succession of heartbreaks.

a succession of 一连串的
- 例 A succession of bad harvest had reduced the small farmer to penury.
连续歉收使得这个小农场主陷入了贫困境地。
Life is a succession of lessons which must be lived to be understood.
人生是一连串的教训，经历了才会理解。

was to be 表示命运，将来必定要发生的事情，翻译成"注定……"
- 例 He came to power, but he was to play dearly for it: soon he was assassinated.
他掌权了，却注定付出了代价：很快他被暗杀了。
They were never to meet again.
他们注定以后永远不会再见面了。

② **The years kept their profound secret, but the day did come.**

did是do的过去式，这里的do表示强调，这种情况下句子中不能有其他助动词。

> Do be careful with that vase!
> 务必小心那个花瓶！

用于表示强调的do可以有时态变化，但其后的动词要用原形。

> He did come but soon went back.
> 他的确来过，但很快就回去了。
> He does speak well.
> 他的确讲得很精彩。

用于强调的do通常只用于现在时和过去时，即只有do，does，did这样的形式，不能用于进行时、完成时等形式。

③ **…he whispered gently, "and nobody ever thought mother less beautiful, did they?"**

该句是反义疑问句，即附加疑问句，表示提问人的看法，没有把握，需要对方赞同。反义疑问句由两部分组成：前一部分是一个陈述句，后一部分是一个简短的疑问句，两部分的人称时态应保持一致。
主要形式：陈述部分肯定式+疑问部分否定式；陈述部分否定式+疑问部分肯定式。
当陈述部分有never, seldom, hardly, few, little, barely, scarcely, nothing, none, rarely, no, not, no one, nobody, neither等否定意义的词时，后面的反义疑问句则为肯定形式。

> He can hardly swim, can he?
> 他几乎不会游泳，对吗？

经典名句 Famous Classics

1. Youth fades; love droops; the leaves of friendship fall. A mother's secret hope outlives them all.
   青春会逝去，爱情会枯萎，友谊的绿叶也会凋零，而一个母亲内心的希望比它们都要长久。

2. The children—they are falling into the hands of the elves; the

smile can make people forget the troubles.
孩子——他们是落入凡间的精灵，他们的笑是可以让人忘记烦恼的。

3. The family you came from isn't as important as the family you are going to have.
你将拥有的家庭比你出身的那个家庭重要。

4. The biggest difference between animals and human beings is that human beings hold the possession of complex emotions.
人类与动物之间最大的区别在于人类拥有复杂的情感。

读书笔记

04 Love Is a Two-way Street
爱，是一条双行道

A father sat at his desk poring over his **monthly** bills when his young son rushed in and announced, "Dad, because this is your birthday and you're 55 years old, I'm going to give you 55 kisses, one for each year!" When the boy started making good on his word, the father **exclaimed**, "Oh, Andrew, don't do it now; I'm too busy!"

The youngster **immediately** fell silent as tears **welled** up in his big blue eyes. Apologetically the father said, "You can finish later."

The boy said nothing but quietly walked away, **disappointment** written over his face. That evening the father said, "Come and finish the kisses now, Andrew!" But the boy didn't respond.

Unfortunately, a few days later after this **incident**, the boy had an accident and was drowned. His **heartbroken** father wrote: "If only I could tell him how much I regret my **thoughtless** words, and could be assured that he knows how much my heart is **aching**."

Love is a two-way street. Any loving act must be warmly accepted or it

父亲坐在办公桌旁，正盯着那些堆积了一个月来的账单，这时，他的小儿子冲了过来，大声宣布："爸爸，因为今天是你五十五岁的生日，我想给你五十五个吻，一年一个！"当男孩正要兑现诺言时，他爸爸大声说道："哦，安德鲁，现在不行，我太忙了！"

小男孩马上不吭声了，蓝色的大眼睛里涌满了泪水。父亲深表歉意地说："过会有空再亲吧。"

男孩什么也没说，只是静静地走开了，失望的表情溢于言表。那天晚上，父亲说："来吧安德鲁，现在可以亲了！"但是，孩子却没有做出回应。

不幸的是，这件事刚过去几天之后，小男孩就不幸溺水身亡。伤心欲绝的爸爸写道："如果我早告诉他，对于那些无心的话我是多么后悔，他一定会明白我的心有多么痛。"

爱，是一条双行道。对于爱的表示一定要热心地接受，

will be taken as rejection and can leave a scar. If we are too busy to give and receive love, we are too busy! Nothing is more important than responding with love to the cry for love from those who are near and **precious** to us. Because there may be no chance at all as in the case of the little boy.

否则对方会以为你拒绝了，从而留下一道伤痕。如果我们忙得连给予和接受爱的时间都没有，那未免也忙得太过分了！对于那些在我们身边，对我们弥足珍贵的人，用爱去回应他们爱的渴望，这最重要不过了！因为如果发生像小男孩这样的情况，即使后悔也没有机会了。

单词解析 Word Analysis

monthly ['mʌnθli] *adj.* 每月的，按月的

例 Many people are now having trouble making their monthly house payments.
现在很多人在支付房款月供上都有困难。

exclaim [iks'kleim] *v.* 突然呼喊，惊叫，大声喊

例 "He went back to the lab", Iris exclaimed impatiently.
"他回实验室去了，"艾里斯不耐烦地大声说。

immediately [ɪ'mi:diətli] *adv.* 立即，马上；直接地

例 He immediately flung himself to the floor.
他立即飞身扑到地上。

well [wel] *v.* 涌出，冒出，流出，溢出

例 He fell back, blood welling from a gash in his thigh.
他向后倒去，鲜血从他大腿上的一个口子里涌了出来。

disappointment [ˌdɪsə'pɔɪntmənt] *n.* 失望，扫兴，沮丧

例 Despite winning the title, their last campaign ended in great disappointment.
尽管赢得了冠军，但他们最后一役却令人大失所望。

Love Is a Two-way Street
爱，是一条双行道

incident ['ɪnsɪdənt] *n.* 事件，事故
- 例 These incidents were the latest in a series of disputes between the two nations.
  这些事件是两国一系列争端中最近发生的几起。

heartbroken ['hɑːtbrəʊkən] *adj.* 极度伤心的，悲痛欲绝的
- 例 Was your daddy heartbroken when they got a divorce?
  他们离婚时你爸爸是不是很伤心？

thoughtless ['θɔːtləs] *adj.* 不顾及他人的，欠考虑的
- 例 It was thoughtless of you to eat all the cake and leave none for me.
  你把蛋糕都吃了，一点也不留给我，这太自私了。

ache ['eɪk] *v.* 疼痛；渴望
- 例 Her head was throbbing and she ached all over.
  她的脑袋嗡嗡作响并且浑身疼痛。

precious ['preʃəs] *adj.* 珍贵的
- 例 After four months in foreign parts, every hour at home was precious.
  在国外待了4个月后，在家的每一刻都是宝贵的。

语法知识点 Grammar Points

① When the boy started making good on his word…

make good 实现/履行（诺言），也可用作"补偿，做出成绩"等。
- 例 He was confident the allies would make good on their pledges.
  他相信盟友们会履行承诺的。
  It may cost several billion rubles to make good the damage.
  也许要花上几十亿卢布才能赔偿这一损失。

类似结构的make短语：make over 转移财产。
- 例 His brother made over the house to him.
  他哥哥把房子转移到了他名下。

② Any loving act must be warmly accepted or it will be taken as rejection and can leave a scar.

be taken as 被当作，被认为是

例 So it may be taken as a typical example of recent work done in this field.
因此，它可以视为这一领域近期工作的典型事例。

There is a danger that comments on Chinese forums will be taken as free thinking or autonomous.
还有一种危险，那就是中国论坛上的评论将会被当作是自由思想或自激。

以上词组后面除了跟as，也可以接to do 或 for。

例 Care must also be taken to prevent silage from being overheat.
另外，还应该注意防止青贮料温度过高。

Proper advantage is not being taken of this splendidly equipped sports hall.
这座设施豪华的体育馆没有被充分地利用起来。

③ There may be no chance at all as in the case of the little boy.

no chance at all 根本不，不可能

例 She might not even find the courage to approach him, and thus have no change at all.
她甚至没有勇气去接近他，因此根本没机会。

Being not fit for the job, he had no chance of getting it at all.
因为不胜任，所以他根本没有可能得到这份工作。

in the case of "就……而言；至于；在……情况下"

例 Poverty depresses most people; in the case of him it was otherwise.
贫穷会把大部分人压垮，但对于他来说，情况可就不同了。

容易混淆的短语是in case of，表"如果，万一或者以防，以备"。

例 In case of failure, their position would be dangerous in the extreme.
万一失败，他们的处境将是很危险的。

The wall was built along the river in case of floods.
沿河筑了堤，以防洪水。

Love Is a Two-way Street
爱，是一条双行道

经典名句 Famous Classics

1. It doesn't matter who my father was; it matters who I remember he was.
   爸爸是什么样的人并不重要，重要的是在我心目中爸爸是什么样的人。

2. We never know the love of the parents until we become parents ourselves.
   不养儿不知父母恩。

3. The family you came from isn't as important as the family you are going to have.
   你将拥有的家庭比你出身的那个家庭重要。

4. The most important thing a father can do for his children is to love their mother.
   一个父亲可以对孩子们所做的最重要的事情就是去爱孩子们的母亲。

5. A wise son brings joy to his father, but a foolish son grief to his mother.
   智慧之子使父亲快乐，愚昧之子使母亲蒙羞。

读书笔记

05 Fatal Suspicion
致命的怀疑

A senior high school student committed **suicide** by jumping from the windows on the fifth floor. The reason was **stunningly** simple: his mother did not trust him.

The boy's father lost his life during a car crash when he was 4 years old. Since then, he lived with his mother and they had been in good relationship. In the winter of the year when the **tragedy** took place, the school required all students to live on campus. The boy's mother helped him settle his accommodation before she left. When she was about home, she found that her wallet was lost. She was **hastily** calling her son, asking him whether he had seen it or not. Her son told her that she had left the wallet on his bed when she left. **Coincidentally,** the boy had no classes in the afternoon, so he brought the wallet back to her mother.

They had agreed to **dine** in a restaurant where they would meet. It was very cold that night. When the boy hurried to the hall of the restaurant, his face was red with cold. The woman took over the wallet and carefully examined

一个高三男生自杀了，他从5楼宿舍的窗户跳了下去，原因令人震惊地简单：竟然是因为他母亲对他的怀疑。

男孩4岁的时候，父亲就在车祸中丧生了。他和母亲相依为命，感情一直很好。悲剧发生的那年冬天，学校要求住校，母亲在宿舍里替儿子张罗好一切后才离开。快到家的时候，她发觉自己的包不见了，急忙打电话问儿子见到她的包没有。儿子说，母亲临走前把包落在了他床上。他下午刚好没课，把包给母亲送过去。

母子俩约好在一家饭店一起吃晚餐。寒风里，儿子赶到饭店大堂的时候，脸被冻得通红。母亲一边带着儿子往餐厅里面走，一边接过钱包，仔细检查包里的每一样东西，看看

Fatal Suspicion 致命的怀疑 05

everything in the wallet to see whether some money had been missing or not when walking into the restaurant with her son.

All of a sudden, the boy halted his steps and said coldly to the woman, "Mum, I am so sorry that I forgot I still have to study tonight, so I've got to go now." Then, the boy quickly disappeared in front of the woman in the icy night.

In the midnight, the woman received a call from the **headmaster** of the school. When she arrived at the school hastily, she could only see his son's **lifeless** icy body.

The last page on the boy's diary before he committed suicide wrote: "My mum did not trust me when I returned the wallet to her. To my sadness, she examined everything inside the wallet to see whether I had stolen her money! The person who loved me most and who I loved most did not trust me! I really could not figure out any sense of living in this world now!"

钱有没有少。

儿子突然停住了脚步，生硬地说："妈，我才想起来晚上还有自习，我得回去了。"说完转身就消失在寒冷的夜里。

午夜，她接到了校长亲自打来的电话，等她匆匆赶到学校的时候，看到的却是儿子冰冷的尸体。

男孩自杀前的最后一页日记上这样写着："我把钱包还给妈妈的时候，她竟然不相信我，她检查了包里的每样东西，看看我有没有偷她的钱，这令我感到难过。世界上最疼我的人、我最爱的妈妈竟然都不相信我！我真不知道活在这个世界上还有什么意思！"

单词解析 *Word Analysis*

suicide ['suːɪsaɪd] *n* 自杀

例 Quite a few have committed social suicide by writing their boring memoirs.
有一些人因为写那些枯燥无味的回忆录而毁了自己的社会形象。

025

stunningly ['stʌnɪŋlɪ] *adv.* 令人震惊地

例 The secret that the priest had confided to him was a stunning piece of news.
神父吐露给他的秘密真是条惊天大新闻。

tragedy ['trædʒədɪ] *n.* 悲剧，不幸

例 They have suffered an enormous personal tragedy.
他们遭逢了巨大的个人不幸。

hastily ['heɪstɪlɪ] *adv.* 匆忙地，仓促地

例 She had married hastily, and as hastily, grown weary of her choice.
她急忙地结了婚并且同样草率地厌倦了自己的选择。

coincidentally [kəʊˌɪnsɪ'dentəlɪ] *adv.* 巧合地，凑巧

例 They immediately got in touch with Dr. Ting who was, purely coincidentally, also in California.
他们立即与丁博士联系，真是巧得很，他也在加利福尼亚。

dine [daɪn] *v.* 吃饭，进餐

例 That night the two men dined at Wilson's club.
那天晚上这两个男人在威尔逊俱乐部进了餐。

headmaster [ˌhed'mɑːstə(r)] *n.* (私立学校)校长

例 Under the wise rule of the headmaster, the school flourished.
在校长明智的管理下，这所中学得以发展起来。

lifeless ['laɪfləs] *adj.* 无生命的；死气沉沉的

例 There was no breathing or pulse and he was lifeless.
没有呼吸，也没有脉搏，他已经死了。

语法知识点 *Grammar Points*

① **The woman took over the wallet and carefully examined everything in the wallet to see whether some money had been missing or not when walking into the restaurant with her son.**

Fatal Suspicion 致命的怀疑 05

take over 接管，接替，文中是"接过来"的意思。

> 例 His widow has taken over the running of his empire, including six London theatres.
> 他的遗孀已接手管理他创下的帝国，其中包括6家伦敦剧院。

whether...or not

除了可以表示"是否"，还可引导让步状语从句，表示"不管是否……"，既可放在句首，也可放在句尾。

> 例 We'll go on with the work, whether we can find the necessary tools or not.
> 我们会继续这件工作，不管能否找到必需的工具。
> You'll have to pay, whether you like it or not.
> 不管你是否喜欢，你都必须得付款。

注意区分"whether or not"和"whether...or not"

whether or not "无论如何，无论"，whether...or not "是否"。

> 例 Whether or not he will never be able to forgive me.
> 无论如何他都不能原谅我。

② **All of a sudden, the boy halted his steps and said coldly to the woman, "Mum, I am so sorry that I forgot I still have to study tonight...**

all of a sudden 突然，冷不防的

> 例 All of a sudden a man fuming with rage rushed in and all the people were frightened out of their wits.
> 忽然一个人从外面气急败坏跑进来，大家都吓坏了。

suddenly "突然地"和 all of a sudden 区别如下：

suddenly 着重于动作没有预兆而突然发生。

> 例 Family values are suddenly the name of the game.
> 家庭价值观突然变得重要起来。

all of a sudden 着重于动作的迅猛程度。

> 例 All of a sudden he was attacked by a robber.
> 突然他遭到一个强盗的袭击。

all of a sudden的用法常放在句首，suddenly的用法比all of a sudden宽。

③ **To my sadness, she examined everything inside the wallet to see whether I had stolen her money!**

to my sadness 令我伤心的是

例 To my sadness, I found my balance was almost zero.
使我伤心的是，账上的余额几乎是零。

to one's +n. 的短语有很多：

to one's advantage 对……有利

例 The present world situation is to our advantage.
目前的世界形势对我们有利。

to one's delight 令人高兴的是

例 To our great delight the day turned out fine.
使我们感到十分高兴的是天气转晴了。

经典名句 Famous Classics

1. People heard the most beautiful voices from mother, from home, from heaven.
   人们听到的最美的声音来自母亲，来自家乡，来自天堂。

2. Losing the loving mother is like flowers in the bottle; although there are color, fragrance, but they lost the roots.
   失去了慈母便像花插在瓶子里，虽然还有色有香，却失去了根。

3. Family is important mainly because it can make the parents get emotional.
   家庭之所以重要，主要是因为它能使父母获得情感。

4. In the world the most beautiful scene is when we miss our mothers.
   人世间最美丽的情景是我们怀念母亲的时候。

5. A real Dad is a man that teaches his child all the things in life he needs to know.
   真正的父亲是孩子的老师，他教给孩子生活中所有他需要知道的事情。

06 Mom Is Child's Angel
妈妈是孩子的守护天使

Once upon a time there was a child ready to be born. So one day he asked god, "They tell me you are sending me to earth tomorrow but how am I going to live there being so small and **helpless**?"

God replied, "Among the many angels, I chose one for you. She will be waiting for you and will take care of you."

But the child wasn't sure he really wanted to go. "But tell me, here in **heaven**, I don't do anything else but sing and smile; that's enough for me to be happy."

"Your **angel** will sing for you and will also smile for you every day. And you will feel your angel's love and be happy."

"And how am I going to be able to understand when people talk to me," the child continued, "If I don't know the language that men talk?"

God patted him on the head and said, "Your angel will tell you the most beautiful and sweet words you will ever hear, and with much **patience** and care, your angel will teach you how to speak."

从前有个孩子即将诞生。有一天，他问上帝："有人告诉我明天你会把我送到人间，但如此弱小无助的我如何在那里生存呢？"

上帝说："众多的天使中，我为你挑选了一个，她会一直等你并会照顾好你。"

但是孩子不确定他是否真的想去。"但是告诉我，这里是天堂，我什么都不需要做，唱歌微笑就行，对我来说，开心就够了。"

"你的天使每天都会为你唱歌，会为你欢笑，你会感受到来自你的天使的爱，你会开心快乐。"

"我如何才能听懂人们说的话呢"，孩子继续问道，"我不懂人们谈论的语言"。

上帝拍了拍他的头，说道："你的天使会跟你说你听过的最漂亮最甜蜜的话语，会非常耐心地教你说话。"

"And what am I going to do when I want to talk to you?"

But god had an answer for that question too. "Your angel will place your hands together and will teach you how to pray."

"I've heard that on the earth there are bad men. Who will protect me?"

"Your angel will **defend** you even if it means risking her life!"

"But I will always be sad because I will not see you anymore," the child continued **warily**.

God smiled on the young one. "Your angel will always talk to you about me and will teach you the way for you to come back to me, even though I will always be next to you."

At that moment there was much **peace** in heaven, but voices from earth could already be heard. The child knew he had to start on his journey very soon. He asked god one more question, softly, "Oh god, if I am about to leave now, please tell me my angel's name."

God touched the child on the shoulder and answered, "Your angel's name is not hard to remember. You will simply call her mommy."

"当我想跟你说话说，我怎么做呢？"

但上帝胸有成竹地说："你的天使会将你的双手合并，教你如何祈祷。"

"我听说人间有很多坏人，谁会保护我呢？"

"你的天使会保护你的，即使冒着她的生命危险！"

孩子小心翼翼地继续说道："但是我会伤心的，因为我将再也看不见你了。"

上帝笑着对孩子说："你的天使会经常和你提起我，会教你回来的路，即使我也会常伴你左右。"

此时，天堂一片宁静，但是人间的声音已可清晰地听见。孩子知道他很快就要启程了，他轻轻地又问了上帝一个问题："上帝，我现在准备离开了，请告诉我的天使的名字吧。"

上帝把手放在小孩的肩上，回答道："你的天使的名字不难记住，你就叫她妈妈。"

单词解析 Word Analysis

helpless ['helpləs] *adj.* 无能的，无助的

例 Parents often feel helpless, knowing that all the cuddles in the world won't stop the tears.
父母经常感到无能为力，因为他们知道无论拥抱多少次也无法止住眼泪。

heaven ['hevn] *n.* 天堂；天国

例 I believed that when I died I would go to heaven and see God.
我相信自己死后会升入天堂，见到上帝。

angel ['eɪndʒl] *n.* 天使

例 Poppa thought her an angel.
爸爸视她为小天使。

patience ['peɪʃns] *n.* 容忍；耐心；忍耐力

例 It was exacting work and required all his patience.
工作很艰巨，需要他有极大的耐心。

defend [dɪ'fend] *v.* 防御；保卫；保护

例 Every man who could fight was now committed to defend the ridge.
每个能够参加战斗的男子现在都决心要保卫这条山脊。

warily ['weərəlɪ] *adv.* 小心地，提防地

例 He looked warily around him, pretending to look after Carrie.
他小心地看了一下四周，假装是在照顾嘉莉。

peace [piːs] *n.* 和平，太平

例 They have been persuaded of the merits of peace.
他们被劝服，认识到了和平的好处。

journey ['dʒɜːnɪ] *n.* 旅行；行程

例 There is an express service from Paris which completes the journey to Bordeaux in under 4 hours.
从巴黎有快车前往波尔多，全程不到4个小时。

语法知识点 *Grammar Points*

① She will be waiting for you and will take care of you.

take care of 照顾，照料，相当于 look after。

例 Don't worry yourself about me, I can take care of myself.
你别担心我，我能照顾好自己。

I believe that neighbors can take care of your son while you are out.
我相信你外出期间你的邻居们会照顾你的儿子的。

take care of 也可作为"保管，保护"解释。

例 The teacher told the students to take care of the new books.
老师告知学生要保护好新书。

take care of 与 look after 都能作"照顾，照料"，可相互替换，但是 look after 没有"保管，保护"的意思。
类似词组：take care 当心，小心。

例 The roses are thorny. Take care not to prick your hands.
玫瑰有刺，小心扎手。

② "I've heard that on the earth there are bad men. Who will protect me?"

on the earth 在地球上

例 Long ago enormous animals lived on the earth.
很久以前地球上生活着巨大的动物。

There are millions of living things on the earth.
世界上有数以百万计的生物。

on the earth 容易和 on earth 混淆。on earth "究竟"，在特殊疑问句中加上 on earth 可以加强语气，表示强调，有很强的感情色彩，"究竟……；到底……"。另外，也可以用 "in the world"。

例 Why on earth do you tell a lie?
你究竟为什么要撒谎？

I've been standing here since half past seven. Where on earth have you been?
我从七点半就一直站在这儿等你，你到底上哪儿去了？

③ **... if I am about to leave now, please tell me my angel's name.**

be about to 表示即将发生的动作，在时间上指最近的将来，一般不加时间状语。

> The school year is about to begin.
> 新学年开学在即。
>
> Hurry up! The train is about to leave.
> 快点，火车快开了。

经典名句 Famous Classics

1. Home is the only hidden place of human shortcomings and failures in the world; it also hides the sweet love.
   家是世界上唯一隐藏缺点和失败的地方，也隐藏着甜蜜的爱。

2. Man's lips can emit the sweetest word: mother; the best call, is "mom".
   人的嘴唇所能发出的最甜美的字眼，就是母亲；最美好的呼唤，就是"妈妈"。

3. Miracles sometimes occur, but one has to work terribly for them.
   奇迹有时候是会发生的，但是你得为之拼命努力。

4. All time is no time when it is past.
   机不可失，时不再来。

5. Time consecrates: what is gray with age becomes religion.
   时间考验一切，经得起时间考验的就为人所信。

6. What I do today is important because I am exchanging a day of my life for it.
   我今天做的事情很重要，因为我为它付了一天的代价。

07 A Letter to Dear Dad on Father's Day
父亲节之日写给父亲的一封信

Dear Dad,

Today I was at the shopping mall and I spent a lot of time reading the Father's Day cards. They all had a special message that in some way or another reflected how I feel about you. Yet as I selected and read, and selected and read again, it occurred to me that not a single card said what I really want to say to you.

You know, Dad, there was a time when we were not only separated by the generation gap but completely **polarized** by it. You stood on one side of the Great Divide and I on the other, father and daughter split apart by age and experience, opinions, hairstyles, cosmetics, clothing, curfews, music, and boys.

Our relationship improved **immensely** when I married a man you liked, and things really turned around when we begin making babies right and left. We didn't have a television set, you know, and we had to **entertain** ourselves somehow. I didn't know what to expect of you and Mom as grandparents but I didn't have to wait long to find out.

亲爱的爸爸：

今天我在商场的时候，我读了好长时间有关"父亲节"的贺卡。那些卡片上面的文字很特别，也或多或少地表达出了我对您的感受。我挑选读过一次后，又挑选读了一遍，但那并不是一张贺卡所能表达出我想对您说的话。

爸爸，您也知道，我们父女俩曾有一段时间因为代沟不在一起，比如年龄、个人阅历、观点、发型、化妆、服装、音乐、作息时间以及男朋友，因为这些，我们的观点非常对立。您站在"大分离"的一端，我站在"大分离"的另一端。

在我嫁了一个您喜欢的女婿后，我们俩之间的关系才缓和了好多。后来，我们为了好好地生个孩子，就离开了，我们之间的那些事情也就结束了。这事您也知道，我们没有电视机看，我们就只好自娱自乐了。我不知道我还能对作为外公外婆的您和妈妈抱什么期望，但是，没等到很久我就找

A Letter to Dear Dad on Father's Day
父亲节之日写给父亲的一封信 07

Those babies adored you then just as they **adore** you now. When I see you with all your grandchildren, I know you've given them the finest gift a grandparent can give. You've given them yourself.

Somewhere along the line, the generation gap **evaporated**. Age separates us now and little else. We agree on most everything, perhaps because we've learned there isn't much worth disagreeing about. However, I would like to mention that fly fishing isn't all you've cracked it up to be, Dad. You can say what you want about wrist action and stance and blah, blah, blah.

I guess what I'm trying to say, Dad, is what every son and daughter wants to say to their Dad today. Honoring a Father on Father's Day is about more than a Dad who brings home a **paycheck**, shares a dinner table, and attends school functions, graduations, and weddings. It isn't even so much about kohlrabi, '54 Chevrolets, and fly-fishing. It's more about **unconditionally** loving children who are **snotty** and stubborn, who know everything and won't listen to anyone. It's about respect and sharing and acceptance and **tolerance** and giving and taking. It's about loving someone more than words can say and it's wishing that it never had

到了答案。过去孩子热爱您，现在他们还像以前那样热爱您。当我看见您和您的外孙在一起的时候，我知道您已经给了他们最好的礼物，您把心都掏给他们了。

就是这样，您我之间的代沟慢慢消失了。现在年龄和其他一些问题的差异把您和我分开，可我们在很多事情上的看法都是一样的，这可能是因为我们明白了没有那么多的事情值得我们争辩吧。然而，我想提示一下的是，爸爸，飞蝇钓鱼是您最喜欢的一种钓法，您可以说些您想做的手腕动作，站姿和一些没有用的话什么的。

爸爸，我想我想要说的话是每个做儿女的今天想和他们爸爸要说的话。过"父亲节"，给父亲这么大一个荣誉，绝不是因为爸爸给家里挣多少钱，和家人一起共进晚餐，参加学校活动，参加毕业典礼和婚礼，也不只是一起栽苤蓝菜，开雪弗莱54和飞蝇钓鱼的事，也不只是您毫无理由地爱那些流鼻涕又很淘气，而且什么都懂，就是不听话的小孩。是因为尊重对方，分享快乐，认同和忍受他人，给予和接受。您对孩子的爱也是不能用言语来表达的，希望这些永

to end.　　　　　　　　　　　　不终止。
　　I love you, Dad.　　　　　　　爸爸，我爱您。

单词解析 Word Analysis

polarize ['pəuləraɪz] *v.* （使）两极化；（使）分化；（使）对立

例 As the car rental industry polarizes, business will go to the bigger companies.
随着汽车租赁业的两极分化，生意将流向较大的公司。

immensely [ɪ'mensli] *adv.* 非常，很

例 Wind surfing can be strenuous but immensely exciting.
风帆冲浪可能紧张吃力，但却非常刺激。

entertain [ˌentə'teɪn] *v.* 使快乐；给……以娱乐；使有兴趣

例 They were entertained by top singers, dancers and celebrities.
顶级歌手、舞蹈演员和名人们给他们带来娱乐。

adore [ə'dɔ:(r)] *v.* 热爱；爱慕；敬慕；崇拜

例 She adored her parents and would do anything to please them.
她很爱自己的父母，为让他们高兴愿意做任何事。

evaporate [ɪ'væpəreɪt] *v.* （使）蒸发；（使）挥发

例 Moisture is drawn to the surface of the fabric so that it evaporates.
湿气被吸到织物表面从而蒸发。

paycheck ['peɪtʃek] *n.* 付薪水的支票，薪水

例 There is an additional five thousand bonus in my paycheck this month.
这个月的薪水多了5000元的奖金。

unconditionally [ˌʌnkən'dɪʃənəlɪ] *adv.* 无条件地

例 The leader of the revolt made an unconditional surrender early this morning.
今天上午早些时候，反叛的首领无条件投降。

A Letter to Dear Dad on Father's Day
父亲节之日写给父亲的一封信 07

snotty ['snɒti] *adj.* 流鼻涕的

例 He suffered from a snotty nose, runny eyes and a slight cough.
他又是流鼻涕，又是流眼泪，还有点咳嗽。

tolerance ['tɒlərəns] *n.* 宽容，容忍

例 He has a sense of humour plus tolerance and patience.
他有幽默感，又能宽容和忍耐。

语法知识点 Grammar Points

① **Today I was at the shopping mall and I spent a lot of time reading the Father's Day cards.**

spend... (in) doing sth. 花费（时间/金钱）做某事，主语是人。

例 They spent two years (in) building this bridge.
造这座桥花了他们两年时间。

spend... on sth. 在……上花费时间（金钱）

例 I spent two hours on this maths problem.
这道数学题花了我两个小时。

spend money for sth. 花钱买……

例 His money was spent for books.
他的钱用来买书了。

② **You stood on one side of the Great Divide and I on the other, father and daughter split apart by age and experience, opinions, hairstyles, cosmetics, clothing, curfews, music, and boys.**

on one side of... 拥护……；站在……一边

例 On one side of the fire sat my mother, and on the other side sat Mr. Murdstone.
火炉的一边坐着我母亲，另一边坐着摩德斯通先生。

On one side of the glass: happy, untroubled people.
在玻璃的一面是快乐和无忧无虑的人民。

split apart 分裂，分开

例 And as for that plan, they are about to be split apart by mistrust and discord.
根据我的计划：他们会被互相的猜疑和意见不合搅得乱七八糟。

③ We agree on most everything, perhaps because we've learned there isn't much worth disagreeing about.

worth doing sth. 做某事是值得的，worth 更像一个介词，所以 worth 后面也可以跟名词、代词、动名词。

例 The good results are worth the efforts.
成绩不错，努力没有白费。
This book is worth reading.
这本书值得一读。
You're worth it!
你配得上这个！

经典名句 Famous Classics

1. What we love is home.
   家是我们所爱的。

2. It is at our mother's knee that we acquire our noblest and truest and highest, but there is seldom any money in them.
   就是在我们母亲的膝上，我们获得了我们的最高尚、最真诚和最远大的理想，但里面很少有任何金钱。

3. Parents know that a caring attitude can not only save you a small fortune, but also even make you feel good about being tightfisted and offering more care than presents.
   父母们知道，关心的态度不仅能帮你们省下一笔可观的钱，而且甚至能使你们感到一份欣慰，因为花钱不多并且给予了孩子们胜过礼物的关怀。

4. The family, life's eternal power.
   亲情，是生命永恒的动力。

08 Never Give Up On the People You Love
绝不要放弃你所爱的人

Like any good mother, when Karen found out that another baby was on the way, she did what she could to help her three-year-old son, Michael, prepare for a new **sibling**. They find out that the new baby is going to be a girl, and day after day, night after night, Michael sings to his sister in mommy's **tummy**.

Finally, Michael's little sister is born. But she is in serious condition. The days inch by. The little girl gets worse. The **pediatric** specialist tells the parents, "There is very little hope. Be prepared for the worst." Karen and her husband contact a local **cemetery** about a burial plot. They have fixed up a special room in their home for the new baby—now they plan a funeral.

Week two in **intensive** care. It looks as if a funeral will come before the week is over. Michael, keeps begging his parents to let him see his sister. "I want to sing to her," he says. Week two in intensive care, it looks as if a funeral will come before the week is over. Michael keeps nagging about singing to his sister, but kids are never allowed in intensive care. But Karen makes up her

像其他的好妈妈一样，当凯伦发现自己又怀孕了时，她就尽力帮她三岁的儿子迈克尔做好准备迎接这个新生儿的到来。他们知道了这是个女孩后，迈克尔每天都趴在妈妈肚子上为他的小妹妹唱歌。

终于，迈克尔的小妹妹降生了，但她的情况很不好。日子一天天过去了，女婴的情况越来越糟。小儿科专家告诉这对父母："希望非常渺茫，请做好最坏的打算吧。"凯伦和她的丈夫联系了当地一家公墓，安排了葬礼的计划。他们已经在家里布置好了一间特别的婴儿房——但现在却要计划一个葬礼。

在重症监护室住了两周之后，小妹妹似乎坚持不了多久了。迈克尔一直乞求父母让他进去看看小妹妹："我想唱歌给她听，"他说。这是重病特护的第二周了，看来好像到不了这周结束，葬礼就要来临了。迈克尔不断地缠着要给小妹妹唱歌听，然而重病特护区不允许儿童入内。不过凯伦

mind. She will take Michael whether they like it or not.

She dresses him in an **oversized** scrub suit and marches him into ICU. He looks like a walking laundry basket, but the head nurse recognizes him as a child and bellows, "Get that kid out of here now! No children are allowed." The mother rises up strong in Karen, and the usually mild-mannered lady glares steel-eyed into the head nurse's face, her lips a firm line. Karen tows Michael to his sister's bedside. He gazes at the tiny infant losing the battle to live. And he begins to sing, in the pure hearted voice of a 3-year-old, Michael sings "You are my sunshine, my only sunshine; you make me happy when skies are gray."

Instantly the baby girl responds. The **pulse** rate becomes calm and steady.

"Keep on singing, Michael." "The other night, dear, as I lay sleeping, I dreamed I held you in my arms……" Michael's little sister relaxes as rest healing rest, seems to sweep over her.

Funeral plans are **scrapped**. The next day—the very next day—the little girl is well enough to go home!

The medical staff just called it a miracle. Karen called it a miracle of god's love!

下定了决心，不管他们愿不愿意，她都要带迈克尔进去。

她给他穿上大号消毒服，快步带他走进ICU病房。他看起来挺像会走的洗衣篮，但还是被护士长给看出来了，护士长大叫，"把那个小孩领出去！这不让小孩进！"一股强烈的母性在凯伦体内应运而生，这位平日里温柔的女性眼睛一眨也不眨地盯着护士长的脸，嘴角显出坚毅的线条。凯伦拉着迈克尔走到他小妹妹的床前。他盯着这个不再为生存而挣扎的小婴儿，开始唱歌。用三岁孩子单纯的心声，迈克尔唱道："你是我的阳光，唯一的阳光，当天空灰暗时，你能使我快乐……"

女婴立刻有了反应，脉搏跳动变得平静而稳定。

"迈克尔，继续唱""亲爱的，那天晚上当我睡着，我梦到我把你抱在怀中……"他的小妹妹放松下来了，仿佛在休息，复原般的休息，似乎在她身上扩展开来。

葬礼计划取消了！第二天——就在第二天——女婴就好起来，可以回家了！

医护人员说这就是一个奇迹，凯伦说它是上帝之爱的奇迹。

Never Give Up On the People You Love
绝不要放弃你所爱的人 08

Never give up on the people you love. Love is so **incredibly** powerful.

决不要放弃你所爱的人，爱的力量奇大无比。

单词解析 Word Analysis

sibling ['sɪblɪŋ] *n.* 兄弟姐妹

- His siblings are mostly in their early twenties.
  他的兄弟姐妹大多二十出头。

tummy ['tʌmi] *n.* 胃，肚子

- Your baby's tummy should feel warm, but not hot.
  你宝宝的肚子摸起来应是暖和的，而不是发烫的。

pediatric [ˌpiːdɪ'ætrɪk] *adj.* 小儿科的

- Pediatric emergency medicine is a rapidly growing area of medicine.
  儿科的急救医学是一个发展迅速的医学领域。

cemetery ['semətri] *n.* 墓地

- The whole area has been shocked by the desecration of the cemetery.
  对墓地的亵渎震惊了整个地区。

intensive [ɪn'tensɪv] *adj.* 加强的；集中的；密集的

- Each counsellor undergoes an intensive training programme before beginning work.
  每个辅导员在上岗前都要接受密集培训。

instantly ['ɪnstəntli] *adv.* 立刻，立即，马上

- He instantly grasped that Stephen was talking about his wife.
  他马上就明白斯蒂芬在说他的妻子。

pulse [pʌls] *n.* 脉搏；脉动

- Mahoney's pulse was racing, and he felt confused.
  马奥尼脉搏跳得很快，他感到很慌乱。

scrap [skˈræp] *v.* 除掉；取消；废弃

例 It had been thought that passport controls would be scrapped.
人们曾认为会放开护照管制。

incredibly [ɪnˈkredəbli] *adv.* 不可思议地；难以置信地

例 It's incredibly heavy.
太沉了！难以置信！

语法知识点 *Grammar Points*

① **Week two in intensive care, it looks as if a funeral will come before the week is over.**

as if 似乎，好像

在 look, seem 等系动词后引导表语从句，使用虚拟语气。

例 She looks as if she were ten years younger.
她看起来好像年轻了十岁。

引导方式状语从句

例 She loves the boy as if she were his mother.
她爱这男孩，就好像她是他的母亲一样。

as if 还可用于省略句中：如果 as if 引导的从句是"主语+系动词"结构，可省略主语和系动词，这样 as if 后就只剩下名词、不定式、形容词（短语）、介词短语或分词。

例 She left the room hurriedly as if (she was) angry.
她匆忙离开房间好像生气了。

② **But Karen makes up her mind. She will take Michael whether they like it or not.**

makes up one's mind 用在好坏立场分明的情况，下定决心。

例 Make up your mind. What time is okay for you?
快点决定，你几点可以？

Did you make up your mind about what you're going to do?
你决定要做什么了吗？

③ **Michael's little sister relaxes as rest healing rest, seems to sweep over her.**

seem to+v.表示不定式的动作发生在主句动词seem之后，比如：

例 It seems to rain.
好像要下雨了。

rain的动作是发生在seem之后的。

例 The beautiful girl's coming seems to scent the air in the hall.
美女的到来，仿佛使空气中增添了香气。

经典名句 Famous Classics

1. He is the happiest, be the King or peasant, who finds peace in his home.
   无论是国王还是农夫，家庭和睦是最幸福的。

2. Maybe you will forget those who shared pleasure with you, but you will remember those who tasted tears with you.
   你也许会忘记那些与你一同笑过的人，但是你将永远记住那些与你一同伤心落泪的人。

3. It is the general rule that all superior men inherit the elements of superiority from their mothers.
   一切优秀的人通常都从他们的母亲那里继承优良的因素。

4. The greatest thing in family life is to take a hint when a hint is intended and not to take a hint when a hint is not intended.
   家庭生活中最重要的不仅是成员之间的心领神会，还需要心有灵犀一点通。

5. A mother's voice is the most beautiful sound in the world.
   世界上有一种最美丽的声音，那便是母亲的呼唤。

09 A Father's Love
父爱

Daddy just didn't know how to show love. It was Mom who held the family together. He just went to work every day and came home; she'd have a list of **sins** we'd committed and he'd **scold** us about them.

Once when I stole a candy bar, he made me take it back and tell the man I stole it and that I'd pay for it. But it was Mom who understood I was just a kid.

I broke my leg once on the playground swing and it was Mom who held me in her arms all the way to the hospital. Dad pulled the car right up to the door of the emergency room and when they asked him to move it, saying the space was **reserved** for **emergency** vehicles, He shouted, "What do you think this is? A tour bus?"

At my birthday parties, Dad always seemed sort of out of place. He just busied himself blowing up balloons, setting up tables, and running errands, it was Mom who carried the cake with the candles on it for me to blow out.

When I **leaf** through picture albums, people always ask, "What does your Dad look like?" "Who knows? He was

爸爸根本不知道怎样表达爱，把这个家维系在一起的人是妈妈。爸爸天天去上班，回家，然后是妈妈向他数落我们所做的一连串错事，爸爸再为了这些事把我们骂一顿。

有一次我偷了一根棒棒糖，爸爸硬是要我送回去，还要我告诉卖糖的人是我偷了糖，并说我愿意赔偿。但妈妈却理解我，她知道我只不过是个孩子。

再有一次，我在操场荡秋千摔坏了腿，一路抱着我到医院的人是妈妈。爸爸将车正好停在急诊室门口。因为那儿是专供急救车停靠的，医院里的人就叫我爸爸把车开走。爸爸大声吼叫起来："你以为这是什么车？难道是旅游车吗？"

在我的生日聚会上，爸爸总显得有点不得其所。他不是忙于吹气球，就是摆桌子，或做些跑腿的活儿。将插着蜡烛的生日蛋糕捧进来让我吹灭的人总是妈妈。

我随便翻阅相册时，别人总会问"你爸爸长什么模

always fiddling around with the camera taking everyone else's picture. I must have a **zillion** pictures of Mom and me smiling together."

I remember when Mom told him to teach me how to ride a bicycle. I told him not to let it go, but he said it was time. I fell and Mom ran to pick me up, but he waved her off. I was so mad I showed him, I got right back on that bike and rode it myself. He didn't even feel embarrassed and just smiled.

When I went to college, Mom did all the writing. He just sent checks and a little note about how great his **lawn** looked now that I wasn't playing football on it.

Whenever I called home, he acted like he wanted to talk, but he always said, "I'll get your mother." When I got married, it was Mom who cried. He just blew his nose loudly and left the room. All my life he said, "Where are you going? What time are you coming home? No, you cannot go."

Daddy just didn't know how to show love, **unless**…

Is it possible he showed it and didn't recognize it?

样？"这还真说不出。他总是摆弄着相机为别人拍照。我和妈妈在一起微笑的照片一定多得都数不清了。

我还记得有一次妈妈叫爸爸教我骑自行车。我叫他扶着车子别松手，他却说是时候了。我摔了下来，妈妈跑来扶我，他却挥手让妈妈走开。我真是气得发疯，决心非要让他看看我的本事不可。我马上骑上车，竟能一个人骑了。爸爸却一点也不尴尬，只是笑笑。

我上大学了，给我的信总是妈妈写的。爸爸只知道寄钱，顶多附上一张便条，告诉我他的草坪现在修整得多么好，而如今我却不能在上面踢球了。

每次我打电话回家，爸爸总像是有话要说，但结果他总是说"我把你妈叫来接"。我结婚的时候，妈妈哭了，爸爸只是大声擤了一下鼻涕，走出了房间。在我一生中，他总是说："你去哪儿？你什么时候回家？不，你不能去。"

爸爸不会表达爱，除非……

爸爸是不是表达了爱，我们却没有意识到？

单词解析 Word Analysis

sins [sinz] *n.* 犯罪，罪过

- Was it the sin of pride to have believed too much in themselves?
  他们过分自信，这是否犯了骄纵之罪？

scold [skəuld] *v.* 训斥；责骂

- Later she scolded her daughter for having talked to her father like that.
  后来她训斥女儿不应该那样对父亲说话。

reserved [rɪ'zɜ:vd] 动词reserve的过去式/过去分词，预订，预留；*adj.* 矜持的，内敛的

- Seats, or sometimes entire tables, were reserved.
  一些散座，有时候是整桌，都被预订了。
- Even though I'm quite a reserved person, I like meeting people.
  我虽然性格极为内敛，但喜欢和人接触。

emergency [i'mɜ:dʒənsi] *n.* 紧急事件，意外事件

- The hospital will cater only for emergencies.
  那家医院只看急诊。

leaf [li:f] *v.* 翻书（报）

- He was leafing a magazine.
  他正在翻阅一本杂志。

zillion ['zɪljən] *n.* 庞大的数字，无法计算的数字

- It's been a zillion years since I've seen her.
  我已经有很多年没见过她了。

lawn [lɔ:n] *n.* 草坪

- They were sitting on the lawn under a large beech tree.
  他们坐在一棵高大的山毛榉树下的草坪上。

unless [ən'les] *conj.* 除非，如果不

- We cannot understand disease unless we understand the person

who has the disease.
若不了解患者，我们就不能了解疾病。

语法知识点 Grammar Points

① **At my birthday parties, Dad always seemed sort of out of place. He just busied himself blowing up balloons, setting up tables, and running errands,**

sort of 相当于副词用法，翻译成"有几分，有点儿，相当"。
- 例 I sort of brushed my hair back with my hand.
  我随便用手把头发往后一捋。

be busy (in) doing sth. 是一个常用搭配，意思是"忙于做某事"，(in) doing 修饰前面的谓语动词 be busy, be busy doing sth. 相当于 be busy with sth.
- 例 We are busy getting ready for this exam.
  我们正忙着为这次考试做准备。
  By the end of this month we will be busy with company's salary report.
  这个月的月底，我们又将忙于做出公司职工的工资报表。

② **I fell and Mom ran to pick me up, but he waved her off.**

wave off 挥手告别
- 例 Hundreds of fans were at Luton airport to wave off their heroes.
  成百上千球迷在卢顿机场向他们的英雄挥手告别。

③ **When I got married, it was Mom who cried. He just blew his nose loudly and left the room.**

blow one's nose 抹鼻涕
- 例 She blew her nose as daintily as possible.
  她尽量文雅地擤了擤鼻涕。

类似的词组
blow one's top 发脾气，大发雷霆
blow one's stack 勃然大怒
blow one's cool 沉不住气
blow one's lines 忘记台词
blow one's lid 发脾气，大发雷霆

经典名句 Famous Classics

1. Time can make people lose everything, but the family is not to give up. Even if one day, the family left, but their love will stay with children in the soul.
   时间可以让人丢失一切，可是亲情是割舍不去的，即使有一天，亲人离去，但他们的爱却永远留在子女灵魂的最深处。

2. Family should be the hall off love, joy and smile.
   家庭应该是爱、欢乐和笑的殿堂。

3. Mild language in the family is indispensable.
   温和的语言是家庭中绝不可缺少的。

4. As a modern parent, I know that it's not how much you give children that counts, it's the love and attention you show on them.
   作为一个现代的父母，我很清楚重要的不是你给了孩子们多少物质的东西，而是你倾注在他们身上的关心和爱。

读书笔记

10 A Father and a Son
父子俩

Passing through the Atlanta airport one morning, I caught one of those trains that take travelers from the main terminal to their boarding gates. Free, **sterile** and **impersonal,** the trains run back and forth all day long. Not many people consider them fun, but on this Saturday I heard **laughter.**

At the front of the first car—looking out the window at the track that lay ahead—were a man and his son.

They had just stopped to let off passengers, and the doors were closing again. "Here we go! Hold on to me tight!" the father said. The boy, about five years old, made sounds of **sheer** delight.

I know we're supposed to avoid making racial distinctions these days, so I hope no one will mind if I mention that most people on the train were white, dressed for business trips or vacations—and that the father and son were black, dressed in clothes that were just about as **inexpensive** as you can buy.

"Look out there!" the father said to his son. "See that pilot? I bet he's walking to his plane." The son craned

一天早晨去亚特兰大机场，我看见一辆列车载着旅客从航空集散站抵达登记处。这类免费列车每天单调、无味地往返其间，没人觉得有趣，但这个周六我却听到了笑声。

在头节车厢的最前面，坐着一个男人和他的儿子，他们正透过窗户观赏着一直往前延伸的铁道。

他们停下来等候旅客下车，之后，车门关上了。"走吧，拉紧我！"父亲说。儿子大约5岁吧，一路喜不自禁。

车上坐的多半是衣冠楚楚，或公差或度假的白人，只有这对黑人父子穿着朴素简单。我知道如今我们不该种族歧视，我希望我这样描述没人介意。

"快看！"父亲对儿子说："看见那位飞行员了吗？我敢肯定是去开飞机的。"儿子伸长脖子看。

下了车后我突然想起还得在航空集散站买点东西，离起飞时间还早，于是我决定再乘车回去。

his neck to look.

As I got off, I remembered something I'd wanted to buy in the **terminal**. I was early for my flight, so I decided to go back.

I did—and just as I was about to reboard the train for my gate, I saw that the man and his son had returned too. I realized then that they hadn't been heading for a flight, but had just been riding the **shuttle**.

"You want to go home now?" The father asked.

"I want to ride some more!"

"More?" the father said, mock-exasperated but clearly pleased. "You're not tired?"

"This is fun!" his son said.

"All right," the father replied, and when a door opened we all got on.

There are parents who can afford to send their children to Europe or Disneyland, and the children turn out rotten. There are parents who live in million-dollar houses and give their children cars and swimming pools, yet something goes wrong.

"Where are all these people going, Daddy?" the son asked.

"All over the world," came the reply. The other people in the airport wee leaving for distant destinations or arriving at the ends of their journeys.

正准备上车的时候，我看到那对父子也来了，我意识到他们不是来乘飞机的，而是特意来坐区间列车的。

爸爸问："你想现在回家吗？"

"我还想再坐一会儿！"

"再坐一会儿！"父亲嗔怪模仿着儿子的语调，"你还不累？"

"真好玩！"儿子说。

"好吧，"父亲说。车门开了，我们都上了车。

我们很多父母有能力送孩子去欧洲，去迪士尼乐园，可孩子还是堕落了，很多父母住豪华别墅，孩子有车有游泳池，可孩子还是学坏了。

"爸爸，这些人去哪儿？"儿子问。

"世界各地"，父亲回答。机场来来往往的人流或准备远行，或刚刚归来，这对父子却在乘坐区间列车，享受着父子间的亲情与陪伴。

这位父亲很在意花上一天陪伴儿子，并在这样一个星期六的早上，提出这个计划。

父母愿意花时间，愿意关注，愿意尽心尽职，这不要花一分钱，可这却是世间无价之宝。

A Father and a Son
父子俩

The father and son, though, were just riding this shuttle together, making it exciting, sharing each other's company.

Here was a father who cared about spending the day with his son and who had come up with this plan on a Saturday morning.

Parents who care enough to spend time, and to pay attention and to try their best. It doesn't cost a cent, yet it is the most **valuable** thing in the world.

The train picked up speed, and the father pointed something out, and the boy laughed again.

火车加速了。父亲指着窗外说着什么，儿子直乐。

单词解析 Word Analysis

sterile ['steraɪl] *adj.* 缺乏新意的

例 Too much time has been wasted in sterile debate.
在毫无新意的辩论上已经浪费了太多时间。

impersonal [ɪm'pɜːsənl] *adj.* 客观的；不受个人感情（或偏见）影响的

例 We must be as impersonal as a surgeon with his knife.
我们必须像外科医生拿手术刀时一样冷静客观，不受任何感情影响。

laughter ['lɑːftə(r)] *n.* 笑声

例 He delivered the line perfectly, and everybody roared with laughter.
那句台词他拿捏得恰到好处，引得众人哈哈大笑。

sheer [ʃɪə(r)] *adj.* （用于强调）纯粹的，完全的，十足的

例 Sheer chance quite often plays an important part in sparking off an idea.
灵感的激发通常纯粹是靠运气。

inexpensive [ˌɪnɪkˈspensɪv] *adj.* 不贵的，便宜的

例 There is a variety of good inexpensive restaurants around that corner.
那个拐角处有很多便宜不贵的餐馆。

terminal [ˈtɜːmɪnl] *n.* 航站楼

例 Plans are underway for a fifth terminal at Heathrow Airport.
在希思罗机场修建第5航站楼的计划正在制定。

shuttle [ˈʃʌtl] *n.* 往来于两地之间的航班(或班车、火车)

例 A courtesy shuttle bus operates between the hotel and the town.
有免费班车往返于酒店和市区。

valuable [ˈvæljuəbl] *adj.* 有价值的，有用的

例 Many of our teachers also have valuable academic links with Heidelberg University.
我们的很多老师也和海德堡大学保持着有益的学术联系。

语法知识点 *Grammar Points*

① **At the front of the first car—looking out the window at the track that lay ahead—were a man and his son.**

at the front of 指在某个物体本身或范围之内的前部，仅指一个点而已，意为"在……前部"。

例 Mike is sitting at the front of the classroom.
迈克坐在教室的前面。（强调教室前面的一点）

in the front of 也指在某个物体本身或范围之内的前部，但范围比at the front of 要大，也意为"在……前部"，两者有时可换用。

例 There is a big desk at/in the front of the classroom.
教室的前面有一张大书桌。

in front of 通常指物体或人位于另外的物体的外部前面。

例 There are some trees in front of the house.
房子的前面有一些树。（树在房子外的前面）

② **I know we're supposed to avoid making racial distinctions these days...**

be supposed to 应该，被期望

例 If you were a lemon, you would not be supposed to dwell on the sweetness of a watermelon.
如果你是一只柠檬，就不该老是盯着西瓜的甜。

Will the au pair be supposed to do light housework?
互惠生需要会做轻体力的家务活吗？

③ **There are parents who can afford to send their children to Europe or Disneyland, and the children turn out rotten.**

turn out作为短语动词，有很多不同意义，其中turn out可以是及物动词，也可以是不及物动词，做"关灯"解时，turn out为及物动词，后面须接宾语。本句中turn out为不及物动词，后接方式状语，意为：to happen, end, or develop in a particular way（以某特定方式发生、结束或发展，翻译成"结果是"。）

例 Despite some initial difficulties, everything turned out well.
虽然开始遇到不少困难，但结局还是不错的。

经典名句 Famous Classics

1. To the world you may be just one person, but to one person you may be the world.
   对于整个世界来说，你可能只是一个人；而对于某个人来讲，你可能意味着整个世界。

2. My mother had a slender, small body, but a large heart—a heart so large that everybody's grief and everybody's joy found welcome in it.
   虽然我的母亲身躯瘦弱、纤细，可她的胸怀却很博大——她可以包容每个人的痛苦和快乐。

3. Children will not remember you for the material things you provided but for the feeling that you cherished them.
   孩子记住你并不是因为你给他提供了多少物质上的东西，而是因为你

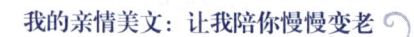

呵护珍爱他时给他带来的感受。

4. A father's love can be compared to a mountain. Although we do not look at it everyday, when you fall down, it's just behind you.
父爱像一座高山，虽然我们不必每天仰望，可是跌倒时，山就在背后。

5. Love triumphs over everything. Love has no age, no limit and no death.
爱可以战胜一切，爱没有寿命，没有极限，也不会死亡。

6. If you cannot hold your children in your arm, please hold them in your heart.
如果你没法将孩子拥在怀里，那就在心里想着他们吧。

读书笔记

11 Promise
永恒的承诺

In 1989 an M8.2 earthquake almost **flattened** America, killing over 30,000 people in less than four minutes. In the midst of **utter devastation** and **chaos**, a father left his wife safely at home and rushed to the school where his son was supposed to be, only to discover that the building was as flat as a pancake.

After the unforgettably initial shock, he remembered the promise he had made to his son: "No matter what, I'll always be there for you!" And tears began to fill his eyes. As he looked at the pile of ruins that once was the school, it looked **hopeless**, but he kept remembering his **commitment** to his son.

He began to direct his attention towards where he walked his son to class at school each morning. Remembering his son's classroom would be in the back right corner of the building; he rushed there and started digging through the ruins.

As he was digging, other helpless parents arrived, clutching their hearts, saying: "My son!" "My daughter!" Other well-meaning parents tried to

1989年，一场8.2级的地震几乎夷平美国，在短短不到4分钟的时间里，夺去了3万多人的生命！在彻底的破坏与混乱之中，有位父亲将他的妻子在家里安顿好后，跑到他儿子就读的学校，而触目所见，却是被夷为平地的校园。

看到这令人伤心的一幕，他想起了曾经对儿子所做的承诺："不论发生什么事，我都会在你身边。"至此，父亲热泪满眶。目睹曾经的学校成为一堆瓦砾，真叫人绝望。但父亲的脑中仍然牢记着他对儿子的诺言。

他开始努力回忆每天早上送儿子上学的必经之路，终于记起儿子的教室应该就在那幢建筑物后面，位于右边的角落里，他跑到那儿，开始在碎石砾中挖掘，搜寻儿子的下落。

当这位父亲正在挖掘时，其他束手无策的学生家长赶到现场，揪心地叫着："我的儿子呀！""我的女儿呀！"一些好意的家长试图把这位父亲劝离现场，告诉他"一切都太

pull him off what was left of the school, saying: "It's too late! They're all dead!" "You can't help!" "Go home! Come on, face reality; there's nothing you can do!"

To each parent he responded with one line: "Are you going to help me now?" And then he continued to dig for his son, stone by stone. The fire chief showed up and tried to pull him off the school's ruins saying, "Fires are breaking out; explosions are happening everywhere. You're in danger. We'll take care of it. Go home." To which this loving, caring American father asked, "Are you going to help me now?"

The police came and said, "You're angry, anxious and it's over. You're endangering others. Go home. We'll handle it!" To which he replied, "Are you going to help me now?" No one helped. **Courageously** he went on alone because he needed to know for himself: "Is my boy alive or is he dead?" He dug for 8 hours...12 hours...24 hours...36 hours...then, in the 38th hour, he pulled back a large stone and heard his son's voice. He screamed his son's name, "ARMAND!" he heard back, "Dad!?! It's me, Dad! I told the other kids not to worry. I told them that if you were alive, you'd save me and when you saved

迟了！他们全死了！""这样做没用的！""回去吧，这样做只会使事情更糟。"

面对种种劝告，这位父亲的回答只有一句话："你们愿意帮我吗？"然后继续进行挖掘工作，在废墟中寻找他的儿子。消防队长出现了，他也试图把这位父亲劝走，对他说："火灾频现，四处都在发生爆炸，你在这里太危险了，这边的事我们会处理，你回家吧！"对此，这位慈爱、关切的父亲仍然回答："你们要帮我吗？"

警察赶到现场，对他说："你现在又气又急，该结束了，你在危及他人，回家吧！我们会处理一切的。"这位父亲依旧回答："你们愿意帮我吗？"然而，人们无动于衷。为了弄清楚儿子是死是活，这位父亲独自一人鼓起勇气，继续进行他的工作。他挖掘了8小时，12小时，24小时，36小时，38小时后，父亲推开了一块巨大的石头，听到了儿子的声音。父亲尖叫着："阿曼德！"儿子的回音听到了："爸爸吗？是我，爸，我告诉其他的小朋友不要着急。我告诉他们如果你活着，你会来救

Promise
永恒的承诺 11

me, they'd be saved. You promised, No matter what happens, I'll always be there for you! You did it, Dad!" "What's going on in there? How is it?" the father asked.

"There are 14 of us left out of 33, Dad. We're scared, hungry, thirsty and thankful you're here. When the building collapsed, it made a **triangle**, and it saved us."

"Come out, boy!"

"No, Dad! Let the other kids out first, because I know you'll get me! No matter what happens, I know you'll always be there for me!"

我的。如果我获救了，他们也就获救了。你答应过我，不论发生什么，我永远都会在你的身边，你做到了，爸！""你那里的情况怎样？"父亲问。

"我们有33个，只有14个活着。爸，我们好害怕，又渴又饿，谢天谢地，你在这儿。教室倒塌时，刚好形成一个三角形的洞，救了我们。"

"快出来吧！儿子！"

"不，爸，让其他小朋友先出来吧！因为我知道你会接我的！不管发生什么事，我知道你永远都会来到我的身边！"

单词解析 Word Analysis

flatten ['flætn] *v.* 使变平，把……弄平；摧毁，弄倒

例 Bombing raids flattened much of the area.
空袭将这个地区的大部分都夷为了平地。

utter ['ʌtə(r)] *adj.* 完全的；彻底的；十足的

例 A feeling of utter helplessness washed over him.
一种全然无助的感觉涌上他的心头。

devastation [ˌdevə'steɪʃn] *n.* （大面积的严重）毁坏，破坏

例 A huge bomb blast brought chaos and devastation to the centre of Belfast yesterday.
昨天一颗威力巨大的炸弹在贝尔法斯特市中心爆炸，引起一片混乱并造成严重破坏。

chaos ['keɪɒs] *n.* 混乱；乱糟糟

例 The world's first transatlantic balloon race ended in chaos last

night.
昨晚世界第一届跨大西洋热气球比赛在一片混乱中收场。

hopeless ['həupləs] *adj.* 不抱希望的；绝望的
例 He had not heard her cry before in this uncontrolled, hopeless way.
他从未听到过她如此绝望地失声痛哭。

commitment [kə'mɪtmənt] *n.* 承诺
例 Work commitments forced her to uproot herself and her son from Reykjavik.
她的工作迫使她和儿子从雷克雅未克搬走。

courageously [kə'reɪdʒəslɪ] *adv.* 勇敢地，无畏地
例 She has courageously continued to lead a fulfilled life.
她一直勇敢地坚持着充实满足的生活。

triangle ['traɪæŋgl] *n.* 三角形物体，三角（形）
例 The place is a cobbled triangle.
这个地方是一块铺石子的三角地。

语法知识点 *Grammar Points*

① ... only to discover that the building was as flat as a pancake.

as…as 和……一样
接形容词或副词的原级，在否定句中，第一个 as 也可换成 so，例如：
例 He doesn't study as [so] hard as his brother.
他学习不如他弟弟努力。
表示涉及数量或程度，可用"as much+不可数名词+as"和"as many+可数名词复数+as"。
例 He doesn't pay as much tax as we do / as us.
他没我们交的税款多。

可用(not) nearly, almost, just, nothing like, exactly, not quite, half, twice, three times, 30 per cent等修饰，并且这些修饰语必须置于第一个as之前，而不能置于其后。

- 例 This room is twice as large as that one.
  这个房间是那个房间的两个大。

② Remembering his son's classroom would be in the back right corner of the building…

in the corner of 在拐角处，文中的back和right用来修饰corner
corner作"拐角"解释，与之搭配的介词，美式英语多用on，英式英语通常用at；corner作角(即180°以内的角)解时与之搭配的介词用in，在……内部的"角"，习惯上用in the corner of...。

- 例 The girl sat in the corner of the classroom.
  那个女孩子坐在教室的角落里。

corner常用的搭配还有at the corner, on the corner, around the corner，例如：

- 例 My brother lives just around the corner.
  我弟弟就住在街的拐角附近。

  The pen is on the corner of the desk.
  那支笔在书桌的角上。

③ Fires are breaking out, explosions are happening everywhere. You're in danger. We'll take care of it. Go home.

break out（战争或疾病）爆发；越狱，逃跑；摆脱（单调刻板的状况）

- 例 He was 29 when the war broke out.
  战争爆发时他才29岁。

  The two men broke out of their cells and cut through a perimeter fence.
  这两个人逃出牢房，并越过了围墙。

  It's taken a long time to break out of my own conventional training.
  我花了很长时间才摆脱掉自身所受的传统训练的羁绊。

经典名句 Famous Classics

1. If you would hit the mark, you must aim a little above it. Every arrow that flies feels the attraction of earth.
   要想射中靶，必须瞄准比靶略为高些，因为脱弦之箭都受到地心引力的影响。

2. If you have great talents, industry will improve them; if you have but moderate abilities, industry will supply their deficiency.
   如果你很有天赋，勤勉会使其更加完善；如果你能力一般，勤勉会补足其缺陷。

3. Live a noble and honest life. Reviving past times in your old age will help you to enjoy your life again.
   过一种高尚而诚实的生活。当你年老时回想起过去，你就能再一次享受人生。

4. Accept what was and what is, and you'll have more positive energy to pursue what will be.
   接受过去和现在的模样，才会有能量去追寻自己的未来。

5. Great works are performed not by strength, but by perseverance.
   完成伟大的事业不在于体力，而在于坚韧不拔的毅力。

读书笔记

12 A Special Letter
一封特殊的信

Dear World:

My son starts school today.

It's going to be strange and new to him for a while, and I wish you would sort of treat him gently.

You see, up to now, he's been king of the roost.

He's been boss of the backyard.

I have always been around to repair his wounds, and to make him calm.

But now—things are going to be different.

This morning, he's going to walk down the front steps, wave his hand and start on his great **adventure** that will probably include wars and tragedy and **sorrow**.

To live his life in the world he has to live in where require faith and love and **courage**.

So, World, I wish you would sort of take him by his young hand and teach him the things he will have to know.

Teach him—but **gently**, if you can.

Teach him that for every **scoundrel** there is a hero; that for every crooked politician there is a **dedicated** leader; that for every enemy there is a friend.

亲爱的世界：

我的儿子今天就要开始上学读书了。

一时之间，他会感觉陌生而又新鲜。我希望你能待他温柔一些。

你明白，到现在为止，他一直是家中的小皇帝。

一直是后院的王者。

我一直在他身旁，忙着为他治疗伤口，哄他开心。

但是现在，一切都将不同了。

今天清晨，他就要走下前门的楼梯，冲我挥手，然后开始他的伟大的历险征程，其间或许有争斗、不幸以及伤痛。

既然活在这个世上，他就需要信念、爱心和勇气。

所以，世界啊，我希望你能够时不时握住他稚嫩的小手，传授他所应当知晓的事情。

教育他吧——而如果可能的话，温柔一些。

教他知道，每有恶人之地，必有豪杰所在；每有奸诈小人，必有献身义士；每见一敌人，必有一友在侧。

Teach him the wonders of books.

Give him quiet time to **ponder** the **eternal** mystery of birds in the sky, bees in the sun, and flowers on the green hill.

Teach him it is far more honorable to fail than to cheat.

Teach him to have faith in his own ideas, even if everyone tells him they are wrong.

Teach him to sell his brawn and brains to the highest bidder, but never to put a price on his heart and soul.

Teach him to close his ears to a **howling** mob...and to stand and fight if he thinks he's right.

Teach him gently, World, but don't coddle him, because only the test of fire makes fine steel.

This is a big order, World, but see what you can do.

He's such a nice little fellow.

教他感受书本的神奇魅力。

给他时间静思大自然中亘古绵传之奥秘：空中的飞鸟，日光里的蜜蜂，青山上的簇簇繁花。

教他知道，失败远比欺骗更为光荣。

教他坚定自我的信念，哪怕人人予以否认。

教他可以最高价付出自己的精力和智慧，但绝不可出卖良心和灵魂。

教他置暴徒的喧嚣于度外……并在自觉正确之时挺身而战。

温柔地教导他吧，世界，但是不要放纵他，因为只有烈火的考验才能炼出真钢。

这一要求甚高，世界，但是请尽你所能。

他是一个如此可爱的小家伙。

单词解析 Word Analysis

adventure [əd'ventʃə(r)] *n.* 冒险；冒险经历；奇遇

例 I set off for a new adventure in the United States on the first day of the new year.
新年第一天，我在美国开始了一次新的冒险。

sorrow ['sɒrəʊ] *n.* 悲哀，伤心，悔恨，惋惜

例 Words cannot express my sorrow.
言语无法表达我的哀伤。

A Special Letter
一封特殊的信 12

courage ['kʌrɪdʒ] *n.* 勇气，勇敢，胆量
- They do not have the courage to apologize for their actions.
  他们没有勇气为自己的行为道歉。

gently ['dʒentli] *adv.* 温柔地，轻轻地，有礼貌地，文雅地
- If your child's temperature rises, sponge her down gently with tepid water.
  如果你孩子的体温上升，就用海绵蘸上温水轻轻地擦拭她的身体。

scoundrel ['skaʊndrəl] *n.* 坏蛋，恶棍
- He is a lying scoundrel!
  他是个无耻的骗子！

dedicated ['dedɪkeɪtɪd] *adj.* 专注的，投入的，热忱的
- Her great-grandfather had clearly been a dedicated and stoical traveller.
  她的曾祖父显然是一位非常投入而且坚忍不拔的旅行爱好者。

ponder ['pɒndə(r)] *v.* 思索，考虑
- The Prime Minister pondered on when to go to the polls.
  首相斟酌着何时前往投票地点。

eternal [ɪ'tɜːnl] *adj.* 永久的，永恒的，永远的
- Whoever believes in Him shall have eternal life.
  所有相信上帝的人都会获得永生。

howling ['haʊlɪŋ] *adj.* 怒号的，猛烈的
- We got stuck in a howling blizzard.
  我们被困在怒号的暴风雪中。

语法知识点 Grammar Points

① **It's going to be strange and new to him for a while, and I wish you would sort of treat him gently.**

for a while 暂时，一小会儿

> She rested for a while, then had a wash and changed her clothes.

她休息了一会儿，然后洗了洗，换了身衣服。

> My words calmed his fears for a while.

我的话使他畏惧的心境暂时安定下来。

sort of 副词性用法，修饰动词，相当于 to some extent, in a certain way, rather, 有几分，有点儿。

> That would sort of ruin the point.

那会有几分破坏的意图。

> I sort of brushed my hair back with my hand.

我随便用手把头发往后一捋。

② **Teach him it is far more honorable to fail than to cheat.**

句子中far的作用是用来修饰honorable这个词，用来说明相比较对象之间的差异程度，属于副词，这种词我们把它称之为形容词比较等级修饰词。

> Housing is a far bigger drag on American job mobility.

住房严重拖累了美国就业的流动性。

比较级的修饰语：常见的有 much, even, rather, still, twice, five times, (by) far, far and away, a lot, a great deal, a little, a bit 等。

> Japanese is much more difficult than English.

日语比英语难多了。（much修饰比较级more difficult）

> She felt a great deal more comfortable now.

她现在感觉舒服多了。（a great deal 修饰比较级 more comfortable）

③ **Teach him to sell his brawn and brains to the highest bidder, but never to put a price on his heart and soul.**

brawn and brains 体力和脑力

> In this job you need both brains and brawn.

做这份工作既劳神又费力。

heart and soul 全心全意

> A dancer must throw herself heart and soul into every performance.

舞蹈演员对每一场演出都必须尽心尽力。

A Special Letter 一封特殊的信 12

经典名句 Famous Classics

1. Don't aim for success if you want it; just do what you love and believe in, and it will come naturally.
   如果你想要成功，不要去追求成功；尽管做你自己热爱的事情并且相信它，成功自然到来。

2. It never will rain roses. When we want to have more roses we must plant trees.
   天上不会掉下玫瑰来，如果想要更多的玫瑰，必须自己种植。

3. No man or woman is worth your tears, and the one who is, won't make you cry.
   没有人值得你流泪，值得让你这么做的人不会让你哭泣。

4. One thorn of experience is worth a whole wilderness of warning.
   一次痛苦的经验抵得上千百次的告诫。

5. Cease to struggle and you cease to live.
   生命不止，奋斗不息。

6. Wisdom in the mind is better than money in the hand.
   脑中有知识，胜过手中有金钱。

7. Storms make trees take deeper roots.
   风暴使树木扎根更深。

读书笔记

13 Mom, I Got My Attitude from You, and That's Not a Bad Thing!
妈妈，这倔劲儿随你，而这不是一件坏事！

Dear Mom,

The big question appalled and surprised parents often ask their child after a **confrontational** or **revelatory** moment is, "Where did you get this attitude from?" I know you hate to admit it, but I get much of my determined and strong-willed nature from you.

Mom, I know it's hard dealing with the teenage angst and the ever-changing moods that come with raising a child. But you should also **marvel** at the fact that I've made it this far, that I'm healthy and happy.

When I was small, I would attend barbecues and family events and wander away from my parents. It wouldn't be long before someone would stop me to ask whether I was my mother's daughter.

"Your mom is Melissa," they'd say, a warm smile on their faces. "Is that right?" I would nod, I assume, parents feel when their child talks back or defies them, I was **appalled** at this statement. To me, I acted nothing like you, Mom.

No one says, "I know you're Melissa's daughter because of your eyes and

亲爱的妈咪，

经过一阵对抗和宣泄之后，震惊的父母通常会问："你的这种态度是哪里来的？"我知道你不乐意承认这些，但我这坚持不懈的性格，大多都是从你那里学来的。

妈妈，我知道为青春期的孩子担忧的感受不好受，也知道你的心情因为养育孩子而跌宕起伏。但你也应该惊叹于我已经成长到了这一步，而我现在健康又快乐。

小时候，我会在烧烤派对和家庭活动中离开父母自己到处跑。不久，总会有人拦住我问我是不是我母亲的女儿。

"你妈妈是梅丽莎，"他们会带着温暖的微笑问，"对吧？"我会点头，我想，当孩子顶撞父母的时候，父母在感情上肯定很受伤吧，我当时被这个想法震惊到了。在我看来，我和你一点都不像啊，妈妈。

没有人会说："我知道你是梅利莎的女儿，是因为你的眼睛和鼻子和你妈妈很像"。

Mom, I Got My Attitude from You, and That's Not a Bad Thing!
妈妈，这倔劲儿随你，而这不是一件坏事！

nose". It's the character **traits** that seal the deal. Dry wit, intelligence, and yes, maybe a little bit of attitude—these are the things I am grateful I have received from you. There's nothing wrong with having attitude.

Like for most black individuals, attitude is what defines you and me, and it's what keeps us from being **mentally** oppressed and defeated. Attitude is a non-violent form of protection and **confrontation**—where would we be in the world without this tool? Surely not where we are.

Mom, when people ask me where I get my attitude from, I tell them: you. And when they ask me where I got my drive, my work **ethic**, my good hair, and my sense of humor, I say you as well. I will always say this.

When I'm asked why I am the way I am—why I refuse to allow others to hurt me with their words or actions, why I think and speak about things openly and without fear—I'll tell them it's because of you.

I'll complain to you about the arguments between us that leave me wondering about how God made us so much alike that we hardly even noticed.

But I'll tell them about you.

Love,

Malahni

其实，性格特点的相似才是背后的原因。我很高兴我从你那遗传了机智、聪明，可能还有一点倔劲儿。这样的性格没有什么不对。

像大多数黑人一样，这倔劲儿是我们的标志，它使我们免于在精神上受到压迫和击败。态度是一种非暴力的自保与对抗，如果没有这个工具，我们的生活将是怎样？肯定没有现在这么好。

妈妈，当人们问我这倔劲儿是从哪来的，我会告诉他们，是从你那儿来的。当他们问我在哪里获得动力、职业道德、我的好发质和幽默感，我也会说是你。我会永远这样说。

当别人问起我为什么会这样处事——我为什么不许别人用言语或者言行伤害我，为什么我可以毫无恐惧地坦然地说出我所想的事——我会告诉他们，是因为你。

我要跟你谈谈我们的那些冲突，它们让我很好奇上帝是如何使我们如此相像，以至于我们几乎没有注意到。

但我会跟别人说，我的优点都来自你。

爱你的

马拉尼

单词解析 Word Analysis

confrontational [ˌkɒnfrʌn'teɪʃnl] *adj.* 挑衅的，对抗的

例 Riot police are on hand but have not been confrontational.
防暴警察随时待命，但还没有出现冲突场面。

revelatory [ˌrevə'leɪtəri] *adj.* 启示性的，揭露性的

例 This paper is revelatory of future study on price dispersion.
本文对未来的价格离散度研究具有一定启示作用。

marvel ['mɑːvl] *v.* 对……感到惊奇

例 Her fellow members marveled at her seemingly infinite energy.
她的同事们对她似乎无穷的精力大为惊叹。

appalled [ə'pɔːld] *adj.* 震惊的，惊恐的，感到厌恶的

例 We are all, of course, appalled that such items are still on sale in the shops.
我们当然对这些物品竟然还在商店里出售表示震惊。

traits [t'reɪts] *n.* 人的个性，显著的特点，特征

例 Creativity is a human trait.
创造力是人类的一种特性。

mentally ['mentəli] *adv.* 脑力的，思考的；心理上，精神上

例 The mental state that had created her psychosis was no longer present.
导致她精神失常的那种心理状态已经消失了。

confrontation [ˌkɒnfrʌn'teɪʃn] *n.* 对抗，冲突

例 They will plead with him to pull back from confrontation.
他们将请求他退出冲突。

ethic ['eθɪk] *n.* 道德规范，伦理

例 Refugee workers said such action was a violation of medical ethics.
难民工作者说那种行为是对医德的亵渎。

Mom, I Got My Attitude from You, and That's Not a Bad Thing!
妈妈，这倔劲儿随你，而这不是一件坏事！

语法知识点 *Grammar Points*

① It wouldn't be long before someone would stop me to ask whether I was my mother's daughter.

It would not be long before 不多久就会……

> The expert predicted that it would not be long before robots replaced humans.
> 那位专家预言：要不了多久机器人会代替人的。

以上句式的原型是It + be + 一段时间 + before…，这样的句型通常使用三种时态：一般将来时，一般过去时和过去将来时，本文中使用的是过去将来时。

It will be+时间段+before 还要过……才……

> It will be three years before his son returns from abroad.
> 要过三年他儿子才从国外回来。

It will not be long before 过不了多久就会……

> It will not be long before he realizes his mistakes.
> 过不了多久，他就会意识到自己的错误。

It was +时间段+ before 过了……才……

> It was a week before I knew the truth.
> 过了一个星期，我才了解真相。

It was not long before 不久就……了；没过多久就……

> It was not long before he told me all about it.
> 没过多久他就把一切告诉我了。

② …why I refuse to allow others to hurt me with their words or actions, why I think and speak about things openly and without fear — I'll tell them it's because of you.

refuse to do sth. 拒绝做某事

> Every time I ask you to give me a hand, you always refuse to do so.
> 每当我需要你的帮助时，你总是拒绝了。

because of是复合介词，其后接名词、代词或者动名词，或者what引导的名词从句，翻译成"由于，因为"。

> I did not go to the cinema because of the intense cold.
> 我因为严寒没出去看电影。
> He lost his job because of his age.
> 由于年龄关系他失去了工作。

经典名句 Famous Classics

1. Keep good men company and you shall be of the number.
   近朱者赤，近墨者黑。

2. Dare and the world always yields. If it beats you sometimes, dare it again and again and it will succumb.
   大胆挑战，世界总会让步。如果有时候你被它打败了，不断地挑战，它总会屈服的。

3. I think success has no rules, but you can learn a lot from failure.
   我认为成功没有定律，但你可从失败中学到很多东西。

4. If you are not inside a house, you do not know about its leaking.
   不在屋里，不知漏雨。

5. There is no such thing as a great talent without great will—power.
   没有伟大的意志力，便没有雄才大略。

读书笔记

14 Mother's Hands
妈妈的双手

Night after night, she came to tuck me in, even long after my childhood years. Following her **longstanding** custom, she'd lean down and push my long hair out of the way, then kiss my forehead.

I don't remember when it first started annoying me—her hands pushing my hair that way. But it did annoy me, for they felt work-worn and rough against my young skin. Finally, one night, I lashed out at her: "Don't do that anymore—your hands are too rough!" She didn't say anything in reply. But never again did my mother close out my day with that familiar expression of her love. Lying awake long afterward, my words haunted me. But pride stifled my **conscience**, and I didn't tell her I was sorry.

Well, the years have passed, and I'm not a little girl anymore. Mom is in her mid-seventies, and those hands I once thought to be so rough are still doing things for me and my family. She's been our doctor, reaching into a medicine cabinet for the **remedy** to calm a young girl's stomach or soothe a boy's scraped knee. She cooks the best fried chicken

夜复一夜，她总是来帮我来盖被子，即使我早已长大。这是妈妈的长期习惯，她总是弯下身来，拨开我的长发，在我的额上一吻。

我不记得从何时起，她拨开我的头发令我非常不耐烦。但的确，我讨厌她长期操劳、粗糙的手摩擦我细嫩的皮肤。最后，一天晚上，我冲她叫："别再这样了，你的手太粗糙了！"她什么也没说。但妈妈再也没有像这样对我表达她的爱。直到很久以后，我还是常想起我的那些话，但自尊占了上风，我没有告诉她我很后悔。

一年年过去，我也不再是一个小女孩，妈妈也有70多岁了，那双我认为很粗糙的手依然为我和我家庭做着事。她是我家的医生，为我女儿在药橱里找胃药或在我儿子擦伤的膝盖上敷药。她能烧出世界上最美味的鸡……将牛仔裤弄干净而我却永远不能……而且可以在任何时候盛出冰激凌。

in the world…gets stains out of blue jeans like I never could… and still insists on dishing out ice cream at any hour of the day or night.

Through the years, my mother's hands have put in **countless** hours of toil, and most of hers were before automatic washers!

Now, my own children are grown and gone. Mom no longer has dad, and on special **occasions,** I find myself drawn next door to spend the night with her. So it was that late on thanksgiving eve, as I drifted into sleep in the bedroom of my youth, a familiar hand **hesitantly** stole across my face to brush the hair from my forehead. Then a kiss, ever so gently, touched my brow.

In my memory, for the thousandth time, I recalled the night my **surly** young voice complained: "Don't do that anymore—your hands are too rough!" catching mom's hand in hand, I blurted out how sorry I was for that night. I thought she'd remember, as I did. But mom didn't know what I was talking about. She had forgotten—and forgiven—long ago.

That night, I fell asleep with a new **appreciation** for my gentle mother and her caring hands. and the guilt I had carried around for so long was nowhere to be found.

这么多年来，妈妈的手做了多少家务！而且在自动洗衣机出现以前她已经操劳了绝大多数时间。

现在，我的孩子都已经长大，离开了家，爸爸去世了，有些时候，我睡在妈妈的隔壁房间。一次感恩节前夕的深夜，我睡在年轻时的卧室里，一只熟悉的手有些犹豫地、悄悄地略过我的脸，从我额头上拨开头发，然后一个吻，轻轻地印在我的眉毛上。

在我的记忆中，无数次，想起那晚我粗暴、年轻的声音："别再这样了，你的手太粗糙了！"抓住妈妈的手，我冲口而出。因为那晚，我是多么后悔。我以为她想起来了，像我一样，但妈妈不知道我在说些什么。她已经在很久以前就忘了这事，并早就原谅了我。

那晚，我带着对温柔母亲和体贴双手的感激入睡，这许多年来我的负罪感消失无踪了。

单词解析 Word Analysis

longstanding [ˌlɒŋˈstændɪŋ] *adj.* 长期存在的；由来已久的

例 They are on the brink of resolving their long-standing dispute over money.
他们很快就能解决长期以来的金钱纠纷。

conscience [ˈkɒnʃəns] *n.* 良心，良知

例 What if he got a guilty conscience and brought it back?
要是他觉得内疚，把东西拿回来了怎么办？

remedy [ˈremədi] *n.* 药品，治疗方法

例 It is natural remedies to help overcome winter infections.
这是有助于治疗冬季传染病的自然疗法。

countless [ˈkaʊntləs] *adj.* 数不清的，无数的

例 She brought joy to countless people through her music.
她用音乐给无数的人带来欢乐。

occasions [əˈkeiʒənz] *n.* 场合，时候

例 Mr. Davis has been asked on a number of occasions.
戴维斯先生曾多次被问及。

hesitantly [ˈhezɪtəntlɪ] *adv.* 迟疑地，踌躇地

例 Watson stared at the photographs, fingering one or two hesitantly.
沃森定眼瞧着这些照片，犹豫不定地指出一两个人。

surly [ˈsɜːli] *adj.* 脾气坏的，不友好的

例 He became surly and rude towards me.
他变得对我粗暴无礼。

appreciation [əˌpriːʃiˈeɪʃn] *n.* 了解，认识

例 They have a stronger appreciation of the importance of economic incentives.
他们对经济激励的重要性有了更深的理解。

语法知识点 *Grammar Points*

① Finally, one night, I lashed out at her, "Don't do that anymore—your hands are too rough!"

lash out at 猛烈抨击

例 In a bitter article he lashed out at his critics.
他写了一篇尖刻的文章，猛烈抨击批评他的人。

② Lying awake long afterward, my words haunted me.

Lying awake long afterward为现在分词用作状语的用法，现在分词作状语可以表示谓语动作所发生的时间、原因、条件、让步、方式、伴随、目的、程度和结果。

例 Being given a chance, she immediately jumped at it.
给了她这个机会，她立刻抓住。（时间状语）

Writing hurriedly as she was, she didn't notice the spelling errors.
因为写得仓促，她没有注意其中的拼写错误。（原因状语）

The little boy went upstairs, trailing his teddy bear behind him.
那小男孩儿走上楼去，还拖着他的玩具熊。（伴随状语）

You gave me such a fright, creeping up on me like that!
你那样不声不响地过来，吓了我一跳。（方式状语）

Granting this to be true, we cannot explain it.
虽然我们承认这是事实，却无法予以说明。（让步状语）

③ I blurted out how sorry I was for that night. I thought she'd remember, as I did. But mom didn't know what I was talking about.

blurt out 突然说出，脱口而出

例 Peter blurted out the news before he considered its effect.
彼得没考虑到后果就脱口把那件消息说了出来。

Then he blurted out almost self-consciously, "but Lee, what am I telling you for?"
突然他几乎是不自觉冲口而出："李，我告诉你这些干什么？"

经典名句 Famous Classics

1. The dictionary is the only place where success comes before work.
   只有在字典中，成功才会出现在工作之前。

2. Until you make peace with who you are, you'll never be content with what you have.
   除非你能和真实的自己和平相处，否则你永远不会对已拥有的东西感到满足。

3. If you would go up high, then use your own legs! Do not let yourselves carried aloft; do not seat yourselves on other people's backs and heads.
   如果你想走到高处，就要使用自己的两条腿！不要让别人把你抬到高处；不要坐在别人的背上和头上。

4. Shallow men believe in luck. Self-trust is the first secret of success.
   肤浅的人相信运气，而成功的第一秘诀是自信。

5. I have no secret of success but hard work.
   除辛勤工作之外，我别无成功的秘诀。

6. A contented mind is the greatest blessing a man can enjoy in this world.
   知足是人生在世最大的幸事。

7. That man is the richest whose pleasure are the cheapest.
   能处处寻求快乐的人才是最富有的人。

8. Will, work and wait are the pyramidal cornerstones for success.
   意志、工作和等待是成功的金字塔的基石。

读书笔记

15 A Letter from Mom to Two Daughters
一位母亲写给女儿的信

Dear girls,

You're so young right now, but I hope these letters will be helpful to you one day when you're older. There is so much I wish I could ask my mother now that I am a **grown** woman. There is so much we never got to talk about. I'm planning on being around for you well into your lives and **adulthood**, but even so, I think having these letters will be useful in some way. Who knows how things might change down the road, and at least you'll have your 34-year-old mother's thoughts down on paper.

Anyway, I want this letter to be about beauty and my relationship to it. I feel this enormous responsibility, as a mother of two little girls, to lead you down a path that is relatively healthy when it comes to beauty and self-image. In a lot of women's eyes I've probably already failed in that respect due to the amount of pink-princess-barbie mess **cluttering** up Vera's room right now.

It's hard for women to maintain a healthy self-image. It's hard not to **obsess** over our weight and to wish we could afford more stylish clothes.

我亲爱的孩子们，

你们现在如此稚嫩，但我希望将来某一天等你们长大了，这封信将会对你们有帮助。作为一个成年女人，我也有很多想问我妈妈的问题，有很多我和她从未谈及过的事情。在你们的成长中，我会在你们身边帮你们过好生活长大成人，但即使这样，我认为这封信也能通过其他方式使你们获益。谁也不知道将来会发生什么，但至少你们会有我这个34岁的母亲把想法写下来供你们参考。

不管怎么样，我希望谈谈关于美以及我对美的看法。作为一个有两个女儿的母亲，在谈到美和自身形象的问题，我有重要的责任为你们引导相对健康的认识之路。虽然在许多女人眼里，我这方面做得并不值得称赞，因为现在在薇拉的房间里还乱糟糟地塞满了卡哇伊的芭比娃娃。

对女人来讲保持健康的形象很不容易。想要不被体重困扰，有能力购买更时尚的衣

A Letter from Mom to Two Daughters
一位母亲写给女儿的信

It's hard not to **covet** someone else's hair or hips or eyelashes, and to spend inordinate amounts of time trying to achieve looks that we were never suited for in the first place.

I have girlfriends around whom I have to brace myself to see, because even though I love them, just being around them makes me **self-conscious**. I look at old pictures of my mother and wonder why I've never been able to be as skinny as she was. And then I have friends who are thinner than their mothers ever were. We women go round and round in circles, holding hands and trying to be one another sometimes.

And I have no doubt that the two of you, Veronica and Juliette, will **endlessly** compare yourselves to each other. You will wonder why one of you got longer legs or shinier hair or bigger breasts or thicker eyelashes. I know this, not because I know sisters, but because I know women. The thing I'll tell you, the thing to remember is this: not even the prettiest of us feel settled. The girl you think looks the most perfect in all the world is probably the girl who wants to change herself more than anyone else.

Don't take these on. Don't let that message carry any weight within yourselves. You are not **worthless**. You

服，这真的很难；不觊觎别的女生的发型、翘臀和睫毛，不在自己身上无节制的花时间试图让自己驾驭那些完全不适合的造型，这些也都太难了。

我身边有一群女性朋友，虽然我很爱她们，但每次跟她们接触我都需要打起精神，只是和她们待在一起我都会觉得不自然。看着我妈妈的老照片，我总是纳闷为什么自己永远不能像她那么骨感，然后我发现身边有朋友比她妈妈年轻时还要瘦。我们女人总在转圈圈，有时还牵着彼此的手试着扮演对方的角色。

毫无疑问，我亲爱的女儿薇拉妮卡和朱丽叶，你们以后也会无止境地相互比较。你们会郁闷为什么对方的腿比自己长，头发比自己亮，胸部比自己丰满或者她有更浓密的睫毛。我懂这些，不是因为我了解姐妹关系，而是我了解女人。我要告诉你们而你们必须牢记的一件事是：即使最漂亮的女人也没有安全感，在你眼里最完美的女孩或许比任何人都想改变自己。

不要太在乎这些，不要让这样的信息增加自己的负担。你有自己独特的价值。你的生

are so full of love and light and you should let it shine through you every second of every day. If someone pushes you down for standing tall then just push yourself back up and stand even taller. And know that the reason they pushed you down in the first place is just because they're scared. I will tell you that I have never in my life felt more beautiful than when I have stood my tallest.

命中充满爱和光芒，让它们每天每分每秒都照耀着你的生活吧！如果有人为了站得高一点而把你推倒，那么你得自己坚强地站起来，让自己站得更高！要知道他们推你下去只是因为他们恐惧。而我要告诉你们的是：当我站在人生最高处的时候，我觉得那是我觉得最美丽的时刻！

单词解析 Word Analysis

grown [grəʊn] *adj.* 成年的，成熟的

例 Few women can understand a grown man's love of sport.
很少有女人能理解一个成年男人对体育的那份热爱。

adulthood ['ædʌlthʊd] *n.* 成年

例 Few people nowadays are able to maintain friendships into adulthood.
如今很少有人能将友谊维持到成年。

clutter ['klʌtə] *v.* 乱堆在，凌乱地塞满

例 Empty soft-drink cans clutter the desks.
空饮料罐胡乱地堆在桌上。

obsess [əb'ses] *v.* （使）着迷；（使）迷恋

例 I must admit that maps obsess me.
我得承认我对地图十分着迷。

covet ['kʌvət] *v.* 渴望，贪求，觊觎

例 She coveted his job so openly that conversations between them were tense.
她毫不隐讳地表示想得到他的工作，以至于他们之间说话都带着火药味。

A Letter from Mom to Two Daughters
一位母亲写给女儿的信

self-conscious ['self'kɒnʃəs] *adj.* 害羞的，难为情的
- I felt a bit self-conscious in my swimming costume.
  我穿着游泳衣觉得有点害羞。

endlessly ['endləslɪ] *adv.* 无止境地，无边无际地，无休止地
- They talked endlessly about beet and cattle feed.
  他们就甜菜和牛饲料的话题谈个没完。

worthless ['wɜːθləs] *adj.* 无价值的，不值钱的；一无是处的
- Training is worthless unless there is proof that it works.
  除非能证明训练有效，否则就是白搭。

语法知识点 Grammar Points

① I feel this enormous responsibility, as a mother of two little girls, to lead you down a path that is relatively healthy when it comes to beauty and self-image.

when it comes 当涉及某事（或做某事）时
- When it comes to getting things done, he's useless.
  一涉及做事，他便不中用了。
  Toddlers are notoriously antisocial when it comes to sharing toys.
  众所周知，刚学会走路的孩子不愿和别人分享玩具。

② ...to spend inordinate amounts of time trying to achieve looks that we were never suited for in the first place.

be suited for 适合，适宜
- He wasn't suited for the job and left after three months.
  他不适合这份工作，三个月后就辞职了。

suit的另外一个用法：suit oneself 随你的便吧，您想怎样就怎样吧。
- -I don't really feel like going out after all.
  我还是不太想出去。
  -Suit yourself.
  随你的便吧。

③ **Don't take these on. Don't let that message carry any weight within yourselves.**

take on 承担，呈现，雇用，录用，文中译为"承担"。

例 No other organization was able or willing to take on the job.
没有任何别的组织有能力或愿意承担此项工作。

Believing he had only a year to live, his writing took on a feverish intensity.
由于以为自己只剩一年的活头，他的文字开始变得激情澎湃。

He's spoken to a publishing firm. They're going to take him on.
他和一家出版公司谈过了，他们打算雇用他。

经典名句 Famous Classics

1. Who strives not when he should strive, who, though young and strong, is given to idleness, who is loose in his purpose and thoughts, and who is lazy-that idler never finds the way to wisdom.
不及时努力学习，年轻力壮时就懒散不堪，生活没有什么目标和思想，怠惰的人永远不能发现智慧之路。

2. Indulge not in heedlessness, and have no intimacy with sensuous delights; for the earnest, meditative person obtains abundant bliss.
不沉湎于放逸，不贪恋感官的享受，具有热忱而且常沉思真理的人，可获得大安乐。

3. Happy indeed we are without hate among the hateful.
在充满愤怒的人群中不怀丝毫的恨意，生活才能够快乐。

4. Happy is virtue till old age; happy is steadfast confidence; happy is the attainment of wisdom; happy is it to do no evil.
到老年还一直保持良好品德的人是快乐的；信心坚固的人也是快乐的；得到智慧的人快乐；不做恶的人也快乐。

5. Happiness consists in the realization of our wishes, and in our having only right desires.
幸福在于愿望的实现，而且在于只存着高尚的愿望。

A Letter from Mom to Two Daughters
一位母亲写给女儿的信

6. One is one's own refuge; who else could be the refuges?
信赖你自己,除了自己之外,还有谁能做你的依靠?

7. Man is the master of his destiny.
人是他自己命运的主人。

8. Health is the best gain; contentment is the best wealth. A trusty friend is the best kinsman; Nirvana (liberation) is the supreme bliss.
健康是最佳的利益;满足是最好的财富。守信的朋友是最好的亲戚;没有烦恼是最大的幸福。

读书笔记

16 Seven Ways to Show Your Love to Your Father
七种方式向父亲表达你的爱

It might seem like your dad will be around forever, but your time together can be cut short when you least expect it. Take advantage of the time you have with your father. Expressions of love are not always easy. They often take **conscious** effort.

"The parent-child relationship is one of the longest-lasting social ties human beings establish," says Kira Birditt, researcher at the Michigan Institute for Social Research. Whether your dad's been in your life all along, or you just recently **rekindled** your relationship, there are many ways to show your dad you love him.

1. Say the words "I love you."

Maybe this phrase was not used much in your home, so it could be tough to **utter** at first. In that case, it's possible your father won't be able to return the **sentiment**. Don't take it personally. The main issue is not to have regrets. Let your dad know what you admire about him and why you're proud. Don't take for granted that he knows.

2. Seek your father's advice and

有时候看上去你的父亲会永远陪在你身边，但当你不经意的时候，你们在一起的时间被缩短了。好好把握与你父亲在一起的时光吧。表达爱有时候并不容易，它们往往需要刻意的努力。

密歇根州社会研究所的研究员基拉·博蒂特曾说过："亲子关系是人类建立维持的最长的社会关系之一。"不管你父亲是一直在你身边，还是你刚刚才重拾这份关系，始终会有很多的方法让你父亲知道你很爱他。

1. 说出那句"我爱你。"

可能这句话在你家里并不会经常使用，所以一开始说出来可能会比较艰难。在这种情况下，可能你的父亲也不会回应相应的情绪。但请不要在意，主要考虑的是不要留有遗憾。请让你的父亲知道你欣赏他的地方和你因他而自豪的理由，不要理所当然地以为他都知道。

2. 寻求你父亲的建议和意见。

Seven Ways to Show Your Love to Your Father
七种方式向父亲表达你的爱

opinions.

This applies from childhood to adulthood. He'll be pleased that you want his guidance. Listen to him. You don't always have to agree, but he will be **flattered** that you asked.

3. Invite your dad into your life.

Introduce him to your friends. Once you leave the nest, welcome him into your new home. When you marry and have children, include your father in many of your family functions.

4. Arrange activities strictly for you and your dad.

Even if it's an activity you might not fully enjoy, share his interests. Let him teach you to play golf or a card game. Take him to dinner, or join him in **outings** with friends and family.

5. Visit your father on a regular basis.

Stop and pick up a cup of coffee to take to him as a surprise treat. Don't wait for his birthday or Father's Day to buy him **thoughtful** little gifts.

6. Inquire about your dad's life.

Ask him to tell you his "old stories" and record them. He will be proud that you care so much, and as a result, you will learn a lot about his childhood and your heritage.

7. Assist your father as he ages.

这一条适用于从童年到成年的时光。如果你寻求他的建议和指导，他会很高兴。请听听他的建议，你不一定总是要同意，但你问他的话他会受宠若惊。

3. 邀请父亲进入你的生活。

把他介绍给你的朋友们。一旦你离开家，请欢迎他加入你的新家。当你结婚和有了小孩时，要把你的父亲当作是你家庭的一部分。

4. 为你和你的父亲特别安排好活动。

即使可能是一个你完全不喜欢的活动，但请你分享他的爱好。让他教你打高尔夫或是桥牌游戏。带他去吃饭，或是和他一起与你的朋友和家人去郊游。

5. 定期地去拜访你的父亲。

放下手上的事情，拿起一杯咖啡去见你的父亲给他个惊喜。不要等到他的生日或是父亲节才给他买个深思熟虑的小礼物去见他。

6. 多打听你父亲的生活。

请求他给你讲他以前的故事并记录下来。他会因为你关心他而感到很骄傲，并且你也可以了解更多的关于他童年和你的祖辈的事情。

7. 随着他年龄增长，你要多帮助他。

Don't treat him like a child. Be patient and understanding. Make sure he can meet his personal care and **medicinal** needs. Help him with his finances, if possible. Take the time to let him know you'll always be there.

不要把他当成个小孩子，要耐心和多理解他。确保他能得到个人护理和药物需求。如果可以的话，在经济方面也多帮助他。多花些时间让他知道你永远都在他身边。

单词解析 Word Analysis

conscious ['kɒnʃəs] *adj.* 注意到的；意识到的

例 He was conscious of the faint, musky aroma of after-shave.
他注意到了须后水淡淡的麝香味。

rekindle [riːˈkɪndl] *v.* 使再燃

例 Ben Brantley's article on Sir Ian McKellen rekindled many memories.
本·布兰特利的那篇关于伊恩·麦凯伦爵士的文章唤起了许多记忆。

utter ['ʌtə(r)] *v.* 发出（声音）；说；讲

例 They departed without uttering a word.
他们一言不发地离开了。

sentiment ['sentɪmənt] *n.* （基于思想或情感的）态度，情绪

例 Public sentiment rapidly turned anti-American.
公众情绪迅速转变，开始反对美国。

flattered ['flætəd] *adj.* （因受重视而）感到满意的，觉得荣幸的

例 I am flattered that they should be so supportive.
他们这么帮忙，我深感荣幸。

outings ['aʊtɪŋz] outing的名词复数（通常指集体）远足，短途旅行

例 One evening, she made a rare outing to the local discotheque.
她有天晚上破天荒地去了一次当地的迪斯科舞厅。

Seven Ways to Show Your Love to Your Father
七种方式向父亲表达你的爱

thoughtful [ˈθɔːtfl] *adj.* 体贴入微的，考虑周到的

例 Thank you. That's very thoughtful of you.
谢谢你，你想的真周到。

medicinal [məˈdɪsɪnl] *adj.* 有疗效的，药用的，治病的

例 Treatment with medicinal herb is attended with good results.
用草药治疗效果良好。

语法知识点 *Grammar Points*

① **It might seem like your dad will be around forever, but your time together can be cut short when you least expect it. Take advantage of the time you have with your father.**

seem like 仿佛……似的

例 Financing your studies may seem like a tall order, but there is plenty of help available.
学费的筹措可能看似一个大难题，好在你可以获得许多帮助。

cut short 缩减，突然停止

例 We had to cut short our holiday because Richard was ill.
因为理查德病了，我们不得不缩短假期。

He cut short his work, put down the cylinder in his hand.
他突然停止了工作，放下了手里的圆筒。

② **Let your dad know what you admire about him and why you're proud. Don't take for granted that he knows.**

take for granted 认为……理所当然，想当然

例 I came into adult life clueless about a lot of things that most people take for granted.
我已成年，却对许多大部分人认为理所当然的事情一窍不通。

Don't take for granted what others do for you. You should be grateful.
不要把别人为你做的事情当作理所当然，你应该心怀感激。

③ **He will be proud that you care so much, and as a result, you will learn a lot about his childhood and your heritage.**

as a result 表示结果，后不跟任何成分，后加逗号。

例 He defeated all competitors and won the scholarship as a result.
他击败了所有的竞争者，最终赢得了奖学金。

经典名句 Famous Classics

1. Though one may live a hundred years with no true insight and self-control, yet better, indeed, is a life of one day for a man who meditates in wisdom.
   假如一个人活了一百岁而没有真实的智慧，又不能自我约束，那倒不如只活了一天，具有智慧和静想的功夫。

2. Sound health is the greatest of gifts; contentedness, greatest of riches; trust, the greatest of qualities.
   健康是最佳的礼物，知足是最大的财富，信心是最好的品德。

3. Let your diet be spare, your wants moderate, your needs few. So, living modestly, with no distracting desires, you will find content.
   过着粗茶淡饭的生活，节制你的欲望，减少你的需要，在这种没有烦虑的适度生活里，你将可以发现满足。

4. Prevention is better than cure.
   预防胜于治疗。

5. Just as the flattery of a friend can pervert, so the insult of an enemy can sometimes correct.
   朋友的谄媚会败坏一个人的品德；同样的道理，敌人的侮辱有时也能矫正你的错误。

6. One should spend reasonably, in proportion to his income, neither too much nor too little. He should not hoard wealth avariciously, nor should he be extravagant.
   一个人用钱应该合理，并且跟他的收入成比例，不可浪费，也不可吝啬；不可处心积虑贪图财富，也不可挥霍奢侈。

Seven Ways to Show Your Love to Your Father
七种方式向父亲表达你的爱

7. Cordial friendship has a supreme taste.
   诚挚的友谊，味道绝佳。

8. Fools, men of little intelligence, give themselves overt negligence, but the wise man protects his diligence as a supreme treasure.
   愚笨无知的人毫无顾忌地恣情放逸；但聪明的却保持努力不懈，视勤奋为无上珍宝。

读书笔记

17 Some Wounds from Mother
来自母亲的疤痕

Some years ago on a hot summer day in south Florida a little boy decided to go for a swim in the old swimming hole behind his house.

In a hurry to dive into the cool water, he ran out the back door, leaving behind shoes, socks, and shirt as he went. He flew into the water, not realizing that as he swam toward the middle of the lake, an **alligator** was swimming toward the **shore**. His mother—in the house was looking out the window—saw the two as they got closer and closer together. In **utter** fear, she ran toward the water, yelling to her son as loudly as she could.

Hearing her voice, the little boy became **alarmed** and made a return to swim to his mother. It was too late. Just as he reached her, the alligator reached him.

From the **dock**, the mother grabbed her little boy by the arms just as the alligator **snatched** his legs. That began an **incredible** tug-of-war between the two. The alligator was much stronger than the mother, but the mother was

几年前的一个炎炎夏日，在美国佛罗里达州南部，有个小男孩为贪图凉快，决定去自家房子后面一个形成已久的深水潭中游泳。

因为迫不及待地想投入到清凉的水中，他飞快地从后门跑了出去，边跑边脱掉鞋子、袜子和衬衣，把它们随手抛在了身后。他一头扎进了水里，丝毫没有意识到自己游往潭中心的同时，一只美洲鳄也正在朝岸边游来。小男孩的母亲当时在屋子里透过窗户向外看着，发现那只美洲鳄正向她的孩子步步逼近。她极度惊恐起来，一边迅速奔向水潭，一边声嘶力竭地朝自己的孩子呼喊着。

听到她的呼喊，小男孩才猛然意识到了危险，立即掉头向岸边的母亲游去。可这时已经无济于事。他的手勉强刚够到他的母亲，鳄鱼也已经接触到了他。

母亲在岸上拼命地拽紧儿子的手臂，而此时美洲鳄也死死地咬住孩子的腿不放。为了争夺小男孩，母亲和鳄鱼之间

Some Wounds from Mother
来自母亲的疤痕

much too passionate to let go. A farmer happened to drive by, heard her screams, raced from his truck, took aim and shot the alligator.

Remarkably, after weeks and weeks in the hospital, the little boy survived. His legs were extremely scarred by the **vicious** attack of the animal and, on his arms, were deep scratches where his mother's fingernails dug into his flesh in her effort to hang on to the son she loved.

The newspaper reporter who interviewed the boy after the **trauma**, asked if he would show him his scars. The boy lifted his pant legs. And then, with obvious pride, he said to the reporter. But look at my arms. I have great scars on my arms, too. I have them because my mom wouldn't let go.

You and I can **identify** with that little boy. We have scars, too. No, not from an alligator, or anything quite so **dramatic**. But, the scars of a painful past. Some of those scars are **unsightly** and have caused us deep regret.

But, some wounds, my friend, are because God has refused to let go. In the midst of your struggle, he's been there holding on to you.

俨然展开了一场让人难以置信的拔河较量。美洲鳄的力气显然要比母亲强大得多，但是母亲挽救儿子的坚定信念让她无论如何也绝不放手。就在这万分危急的关头，一位农夫恰巧驾车经过，一听到孩子母亲的尖叫便飞速从卡车上跳下，瞄准鳄鱼并开枪将其射杀。

值得庆幸的是，在医院经过数周的抢救治疗，小男孩居然存活了下来。鳄鱼凶残的袭击在他的腿上刻下了触目惊心的伤痕。不仅如此，他的双臂上也留下了深深的抓痕，那是在生死关头母亲为了牢牢抓住挚爱的儿子，以至于手指甲都掐入了儿子的肉中所留下的。

事后，这位死里逃生的小男孩接受了一位报社记者的采访。当记者问他是否愿意让大家看看他身上的伤疤时，小男孩挽起了自己的裤腿，腿上深深的疤痕暴露无遗。紧接着，他满脸自豪地告诉记者，"大家还是看看我的手臂吧，我的手臂上也有好多伤疤呢。这是妈妈不放开我，在救我的时候留下的。"

看了这个小男孩的故事后，人们都能感同身受。其实我们每个人身上都有伤疤。只不过并不是被鳄鱼咬的，或任何如此戏剧性事件所造成，而是过往的痛苦经历所留下的。那些伤疤是如此难看，让人深感懊悔。

但是，我的朋友，你可曾想过有些伤口是一些不想放弃你的人造成的。在你挣扎的过程中，那些爱你的人为了拉住你，才在你身上留下了这些伤疤。

单词解析 Word Analysis

alligator ['ælɪgeɪtə(r)] *n.* 短吻鳄

例 He was grappling with an alligator in a lagoon.
他正在环礁湖里与一只短吻鳄搏斗。

shore [ʃɔː(r)] *n.* 海岸，河岸，湖滨

例 They walked down to the shore.
他们走到了湖边。

utter ['ʌtə(r)] *adj.* 完全的，彻底的

例 A look of utter confusion swept across his handsome face.
他英俊的脸上掠过一丝大惑不解的神情。

alarmed [ə'lɑːmd] *adj.* 惊恐的；忧虑的；担心的

例 They should not be too alarmed by the press reports.
对于新闻报道他们不应过于担心。

dock [dɒk] *n.* 码头，船坞

例 She headed for the docks, thinking that Ricardo might be hiding in one of the boats.
她走向码头，想着里卡多可能正藏在其中一条船上。

snatch [snætʃ] *v.* 一把抓住，迅速地夺取

例 He snatched up the telephone.
他迅速地抓起了话筒。

Some Wounds from Mother
来自母亲的疤痕 17

incredible [ɪnˈkredəbl] *adj.* 不可思议的，难以置信的

例 It seemed incredible that people would still want to play football during a war.
在战时人们仍然想踢足球，这似乎不可思议。

vicious [ˈvɪʃəs] *adj.* 残暴的，凶残的，凶恶的

例 He suffered a vicious attack by a gang of white youths.
他遭到一帮白人青年的残暴袭击。

trauma [ˈtrɔːmə] *n.* 精神创伤，惊骇（或痛苦）的经历

例 The officers are claiming compensation for trauma after the disaster.
灾难过后军官们正在要求赔偿精神损失。

identify [aɪˈdentɪfaɪ] *v.* 识别，分辨出

例 I tried to identify her perfume.
我试图分辨出她用哪种香水。

dramatic [drəˈmætɪk] *adj.* 突如其来的，急剧的

例 This policy has led to a dramatic increase in our prison populations.
这项政策已经让我们监狱的囚犯人数激增。

unsightly [ʌnˈsaɪtli] *adj.* 难看的，不悦目的，不雅观的

例 My mother has had unsightly varicose veins for years.
我母亲多年来一直患有难看的静脉曲张。

语法知识点 Grammar Points

① **His mother—in the house was looking out the window—saw the two as they got closer and closer together.**

closer and closer 越来越近，这是比较级and比较级的用法，表示"越……越……"，and连接同一个形容词的比较级。若比较级是原级+er构成的，则常用比较级 + and + 比较级形式；若比较级是more + 原级构成的，需用more and more + 原级形式。

例 Our city becomes cleaner and cleaner.
我们的城市变得越来越干净。
He does his homework more and more carefully.
他做作业越来越认真了。

另外一个关于比较级的常用用法是，从句：the + 比较级，主句：the + 比较级。

例 The longer the treatment is delayed, the worse the prognosis will be.
延误治疗的时间越长，预后越差。
The more we study, the more we discover our ignorance.
我们越学习，就越发现自己无知。

② **A farmer happened to drive by, heard her screams, raced from his truck, took aim and shot the alligator.**

happen to 某人碰巧做某事；某人出了某事（常指不好的事）

例 A car accident happened to her this morning.
今天上午她发生了交通事故。
I happened to meet a friend of mine in the street yesterday.
昨天我碰巧在街上遇到了我的一个朋友。

表示"碰巧或恰巧发生某事"时，还可用"It happens / happened that…"这一结构来表达。

例 It happened that he had to take part in a meeting that afternoon.
碰巧那天下午他不得不参加一个会议。

经典名句 Famous Classics

1. You cannot improve your past, but you can improve your future. Once time is wasted, life is wasted.
   你不能改变你的过去，但你可以让你的未来变得更美好。一旦时间浪费了，生命就浪费了。

2. Knowledge can change your fate and English can accomplish your future.
   知识改变命运，英语成就未来。

Some Wounds from Mother
来自母亲的疤痕

3. Make haste in doing good; restrain your mind from evil. Whosoever is slow in doing well, his mind delights in evil.
及时行善，以免你的心里再起坏念头。凡是不能及时行善的人，内心常会生起恶念。

4. Be tolerant among the intolerant, gentle among the violent, and free from greed among the greedy.
在急躁的人中要容忍，在凶暴的人中要温和，在贪婪的人中要慷慨。

5. As a beautiful flower that is full of hue but lacks fragrance, even so fruitless is the well-spoken word of one who does not practice it.
只说好话而没有实行是毫无结果的，这好比一朵美丽的花，徒具颜色而没有芳香。

读书笔记

18 What Do Parents Owe Their Children?
父母到底欠子女什么？

If I had to select a word that best describes the **majority** of parents in China, that word would be **guilt-ridden**. How sad it is to see parents become the willing **victims** of the "give-me game", only to discover that, no matter what they do, it isn't enough. In the end, they are despised for their lack of firmness and blamed when their spoiled children get in trouble. With this in mind, I shall first answer this question: "What do parents **owe** their children?" and I shall start with what they don't owe them.

Parents don't owe their children every minute of their day and every ounce of their energy. They don't owe them round-the-clock car service, singing lessons, tennis lessons, expensive bicycles, a motorcycle or a car when they reach eighteen.

I take the firm position that parents do not owe their children a college education. If they can afford it, they can certainly send them to the best universities. But they must not feel **guilty** if they can't. If the children really want to go, they'll find a way. There are plenty of loans and scholarships for the

如果我必须挑选取一个词，来恰当描述中国的大多数父母，这个词便是"内疚"。目睹父母们甘愿做"给我游戏"的牺牲者是很令人伤心的。但我们发现无论他们怎么做，都还是不够。到最后，父母们都会因自己的软弱而受到蔑视，因他们宠坏的孩子惹出事端而受到责备。认识到这些，我们应该首先回答这个问题："父母欠子女些什么？"而我首先要从他们不欠子女什么谈起。

父母不必把分分秒秒的时间、点点滴滴的精力都花在孩子们身上。不必时时准备替他们开车外出，不必让他们上音乐课和网球课，不必给他们买很贵的自行车、摩托车，或在他们满十八岁时给他们买车。

我还确信父母并不欠孩子高等教育的费用。如果付得起，很好，他们当然可以将子女送进一流大学。但付不起亦无须感到愧疚。假如子女们真愿意上大学，他们自己会找到办法。因为有许多为聪明好学

What Do Parents Owe Their Children?
父母到底欠子女什么？ 18

bright and eager who can't afford to pay.

After children marry, their parents do not owe them a down payment on a house or money for the furniture. They do not have an **obligation** to baby-sit or to take their grandchildren in their house when the parents were on vacation. If they want to do it, it must be considered a favor, not an obligation.

In my opinion, parents do not owe their children an **inheritance**, no matter how much money they have. One of the surest ways to produce a **loafer** is to let children know that their future is assured.

No child asks to be born. If you bring a life into the world, you owe the children something. And if you give him his **due**, he'll have something of value to pass along to your grandchildren.

而又无力支付学费的年轻人设立的贷款项目和奖学金。

孩子结婚后，父母无须为他们分期付款买房子而出首付款，无须为他们购买家具，也不一定要照顾孙辈，或是在子女度假时看管孙儿、孙女。倘若父母乐意这么做，子女应把这看作恩惠而不是义务。

在我看来，无论父母多么有钱，都不一定要给子女一笔遗产。让子女知道自己前途已有保障，无疑最能使他们变为懒虫。

没有任何孩子是自己要求出世的。倘若你将一个生命带到世界上来，你便对他负有义务。如果你给予了他应得的，他也将会把一些有价值的东西传给你的孙辈们。

单词解析 Word Analysis

majority [mə'dʒɒrəti] *n.* 大多数，多数

例 The majority of my patients come to me from out of town.
大多数来找我看病的患者都是外省人。

guilt-ridden ['gɪltr'ɪdn] *adj.* 有负罪感的；深感歉疚的

例 She was guilt-ridden at the way she had treated him.
她为过去那样对待他而深感内疚。

victim ['vɪktɪm] *n.* 受害者，遇害者，遇难者

例 Not all the victims survived.
并非所有受害者都得以幸存。

owe [əʊ] *v.* 欠（钱）；欠（债）；欠（账）

例 The company owes money to more than 60 banks.
这家公司欠下60多家银行的债。

guilty ['gɪltɪ] *adj.* 内疚的；感到愧疚的

例 When she saw me she looked guilty.
她见到我时一脸歉疚。

obligation [ˌɒblɪ'geɪʃn] *n.* 义务；责任

例 When teachers assign homework, students usually feel an obligation to do it.
老师布置作业时，学生通常认为完成作业是一种义务。

inheritance [ɪn'herɪtəns] *n.* 遗产，继承物

例 She feared losing her inheritance to her stepmother.
她担心她继承的遗产会被继母夺走。

loafer ['ləʊfə(r)] *n.* 游手好闲，无业游民

例 From the sound of it, it was the voice of Lu, the well-known loafer.
听声音就知道是本街有名的闲汉陆和尚。

语法知识点 Grammar Points

① **In the end, they are despised for their lack of firmness and blamed when their spoiled children get in trouble.**

lack of 由于缺乏……，这里的lack是名词，绝对不能与for连用。

例 She didn't attend the party for lack of confidence.
她没有参加这个聚会，因为她没有信心。

be lacking in 也表示缺乏，lacking作形容词用，前面有系动词，后面与in搭配使用。

例 She is lacking in confidence.
她没有信心。

lack 作不及物动词，用于否定句中。

例 She doesn't lack for confidence.
她不缺乏信心。

② There are plenty of loans and scholarships for the bright and eager who can't afford to pay.

plenty of 大量的，充足的，其后跟可数名词与不可数名词均可。

例 He indulges his son with plenty of pocket money.
他纵容他的儿子，给他许多零用钱。
The new collections of custom furs around town reveal plenty of folderol, but there are practical things too.
市上大批新的定做的皮衣中有许多是华而不实的，但也有一些实用的东西。

plenty of 同义的词组还有 a great deal of, a lot of 等。
a great deal of 大量，很多，后接不可数名词，谓语动词用单数。

例 A great deal of money was spent on wasteful things.
花了大笔的钱在无用的事情上。

a lot of 许多，通常用于口语，后接可数或不可数名词，谓语动词用单数或复数视后接的名词而定。

例 She seems to run into a lot of trouble at her job.
她在工作上似乎遇到了许多麻烦。

经典名句 *Famous Classics*

1. Better than a thousand utterance with useless word is one single beneficial word, by hearing which one is pacified.
读诵没有用的话语一千句，倒不如只听到一句有益的话带给人安宁。

2. One should not pry into the faults of others, into things done and left undone by others. One should rather consider what by oneself is done and left undone.
不应挑剔别人的过失，批评别人已做和未做的事情。应时常反省自己的过失，考虑自己所做和未做的事情。

3. One should make his speeches free from caustic remarks against

others.
一个人言谈时，应避免以尖酸刻薄的话去批评别人。

4. The words of a man who is reserved in his speech and talks wisely and rationally are delightful to the ear.
讲话有分寸，谈吐婉转、言之有理，那么你讲的话就会美妙动听。

5. With the intelligent, the wise, the learned, the devout and the dutiful—with such a virtuous, intellectual man should one associate.
要常亲近贤明的人、有智慧的人、博学的人、忠诚热心的人、尽责的人——常跟这些智德兼备的人来往。

6. Be fond of sleep, fond of company, indolent, lazy and irritable-this is a cause of one's downfall.
贪睡眠，爱闲聊，对所学的东西不感兴趣，做事情懒懒散散，急躁而没有耐心……是导致堕落的重大要素。

7. Without learning, men grow as cows do increasing only in flesh not wisdom.
不学习的人，宛如老牛，肉虽多，却没有智慧。

读书笔记

19 Run Through the Rain
雨中的记忆

She had been shopping with her Mom in Wal-Mart. She must have been 6 years old, this beautiful brown haired, freckle-faced image of innocence. It was pouring outside. The kind of rain that gushes over the top of rain gutters, so much in a hurry to hit the Earth, it has no time to flow down the **spout**.

We all stood there under the **awning** and just inside the door of the Wal-Mart. We all waited, some patiently, others irritated, because nature messed up their hurried day. I am always **mesmerized** by rainfall. I get lost in the sound and sight of the heavens washing away the dirt and dust of the world. Memories of running, splashing so **carefree** as a child come pouring in as a welcome **reprieve** from the worries of my day.

Her voice was so sweet as it broke the hypnotic trance we were all caught in, "Mom, let's run through the rain." she said.

"No, honey. We'll wait until it slows down a bit." Mom replied.

This young child waited about another minute and repeated: "Mom, let's run through the rain."

她和妈妈刚在沃尔玛结束购物。这个天真的小女孩应该6岁大了，头发是美丽的棕色，脸上有雀斑。外面下着倾盆大雨。雨水溢满了檐槽，来不及排走，就迫不及待地涌涨上地面。

我们都站在沃尔玛门口的遮篷下。大家都在等待，有人很耐心，有人很烦躁，因为老天在给他们本已忙碌的一天添乱。雨天总引起我的遐思。我出神地听着、看着老天冲刷洗涤这世界的污垢和尘埃，孩时无忧无虑地在雨中奔跑玩水的记忆汹涌而至，暂时缓解了我一天的焦虑。

小女孩甜美的声音打破了这令人昏昏欲睡的气氛，"妈妈，我们在雨里跑吧。"她说。

"不，亲爱的，我们等雨小一点再走。"母亲回答说。

过了一会小女孩又说："妈妈，我们跑出去吧。"

"这样的话我们会湿透的。"母亲说。

"不会的，妈妈。你今天

"We'll get soaked if we do." Mom said.

"No, we won't, Mom. That's not what you said this morning," the young girl said as she **tugged** at her Mom's arm.

"This morning? When did I say we could run through the rain and not get wet?"

"Don't you remember? When you were talking to Daddy about his cancer, you said, If God can get us through this, he can get us through anything!"

Now some would laugh it off and scold her for being silly. Some might even ignore what was said. But this was a moment of **affirmation** in a young child's life. Time when **innocent** trust can be **nurtured** so that it will bloom into faith. "Honey, you are absolutely right. Let's run through the rain. If we get wet, well maybe we just needed washing." Mom said. Then off they ran.

We all stood watching, smiling and laughing as they darted past the cars. They held their shopping bags over their heads just in case. They got soaked. But they were followed by a few who screamed and laughed like children all the way to their cars. And yes, I did. I ran. I got wet. I needed washing. Circumstances or people can take away

早上不是这样说的。"小女孩一边说，一边拉着母亲的手。

"今天早上？我什么时候说过我们淋雨不会湿啊？"

"你不记得了吗？你和爸爸谈他的癌症时，你不是说'如果上帝让我们闯过这一关，那我们就没有什么过不去。'"

有人也许会对此一笑了之，或者责备这孩子的不懂事，有人甚至不把她的话放在心上。但这却是一个小孩子一生中需要被肯定的时候。若受到鼓舞，此时孩子单纯的信任就会发展成为坚定的信念。"亲爱的，你说得对，我们跑过去吧。如果淋湿了，那也许是因为我们的确需要冲洗一下了。"母亲说。然后她们就冲出去了。

我们站在那里，笑着看她们飞快地跑过停着的汽车。她们把购物袋高举过头想挡挡雨，但还是湿透了。好几个人像孩子般尖叫着，大笑着，也跟着冲了出去，奔向自己的车子。当然，我也这样做了，跑了出去，淋湿了。我也需要接受洗礼。环境或其他人可以夺去你的物质财富，抢走你的金钱，带走你的健康，但没有

Run Through the Rain
雨中的记忆 19

your material possessions, they can take away your money, and they can take away your health. But no one can ever take away your precious memories. So, don't forget to make time and take the opportunities to make memories every day!

To everything there is a season and a time to every purpose under heaven. I hope you still take the time to run through the rain.

人可以带走你珍贵的回忆。因此，记得要抓紧时间，抓住机会每天都给自己留下一些回忆吧。

世间万物皆有自己的季节，做任何事情也有一个恰当的时机。希望你有机会在雨中狂奔一回。

单词解析 Word Analysis

spout [spaʊt] *n.* （迅速喷出的）液流，水柱

例 Rain from the roof goes down a long spout.
屋顶上的雨水从一条漏水的管子中流出来。

awning [ˈɔːnɪŋ] *n.* 遮阳篷，雨棚

例 Several people herded under an awning to get out the shower.
几个人聚集在门栅下避阵雨。

mesmerize [ˈmezməˌraɪz] *v.* 使入迷

例 He was absolutely mesmerized by Pavarotti on television.
他完全被电视上的帕瓦罗蒂迷住了。

carefree [ˈkeəfriː] *adj.* 无忧无虑的，毫无牵挂的

例 Chantal remembered carefree past summers at the beach.
钱特尔记起了从前在海滩上度过的无忧无虑的夏日时光。

reprieve [rɪˈpriːv] *n.* （不好或艰难情况的）暂缓，延缓

例 It looked as though the college would have to shut, but this week it was given a reprieve.
这所大学看起来要关闭了，但这周情况暂时有所缓解。

tug [tʌg] *v.* 使劲拉，拽

例 A little boy came running up and tugged at his sleeve excitedly.
一个小男孩跑上来，非常激动地拽着他的袖子。

affirmation [ˌæfəˈmeɪʃn] *n.* 肯定，确认

例 The desirability of peace needs no affirmation.
和平的可取无容赘言。

innocent [ˈɪnəsnt] *adj.* 天真的，不谙世故

例 He's curiously innocent about what this means to other people.
关于这对其他人意味着什么，他一无所知，这一点颇不寻常。

nurture [ˈnɜːtʃə] *v.* 养育

例 Parents want to know the best way to nurture and raise their child to adulthood.
父母希望知道养育孩子长大成人的最佳方法。

语法知识点 *Grammar Points*

① **She had been shopping with her Mom in Wal-Mart. She must have been 6 years old.**

must have done 表示对过去事情的肯定推测，译成"一定做过某事"，该结构用于肯定句。

例 It must have rained last night, for the ground is wet.
昨晚一定下雨了，因为地面还是湿的。

You must have been mad to speak to the servant.
你和仆人说话，一定是发疯了。

如果 must + have + 过去分词与 by now 连用，还可以表示对现在完成的动作和状态的肯定推测，但实质上还是指所推测的过去的动作。

例 They started early this morning; they must have arrived by now.
他们今晨很早就出发了，现在肯定已经到了。

② **Now some would laugh it off and scold her for being silly.**

laugh sth. off 对……一笑置之

Run Through the Rain
雨中的记忆 19

例 She tried to laugh off their remarks, but I could see she was hurt.
她试图对他们的话一笑置之，但我看得出她的内心还是受到了伤害。

laugh相关的短语：laugh in sb.'s face 当某人的面嘲笑
laugh at sb./sth. 取笑（某人），笑话（某人）

例 They'd laugh in your face if you suggested me for the post.
如果你提议让我担任这个职位，他们准会当面嘲笑你。

I can't go into work looking like this—everyone will laugh at me.
我不能这个样子去上班——大家会笑话我的。

③ **But no one can ever take away your precious memories. So, don't forget to make time and take the opportunities to make memories every day!**

take away 拿走，夺走；解除，消除

例 In prison they'd taken away all his possessions.
在监狱里，他们夺走了他所有的财物。

Have a sweet to take away the taste.
吃一块糖来去除这个味道。

经典名句 Famous Classics

1. Great hopes make great man.
   伟大的理想造就伟大的人。

2. A strong man will struggle with the storms of fate.
   强者能同命运的风暴抗争。

3. Live a noble and honest life. Reviving past times in your old age will help you to enjoy your life again.
   过一种高尚而诚实的生活。当你年老时回想起过去，你就能再一次享受人生。

4. Behind every successful man there's a lot of unsuccessful years.
   每个成功者的后面都有很多不成功的岁月。

5. Enrich your life today. Yesterday is history. Tomorrow is mystery.
   充实今朝，昨日已成过去，明天充满神奇。

20 Not a Simple Dress
不凡的连衣裙

"Do you like my dress?" she asked of a passing stranger.

"My mommy made it just for me." She said with a tear in her eyes.

"Well, I think it's very pretty, so tell me little one, why are you crying?"

With a **quiver** in her voice the little girl answered. "After Mommy made me this dress, she had to go away."

Well, now, said the lady, "With a little girl like you waiting for her, I'm sure she'll be right back."

"No Ma'am, you don't understand," said the child through her tears, "My daddy said she's up in heaven now with Grandfather."

Finally the woman realized what the child meant, and why she was crying. **Kneeling** down she gently **cradled** the child in her arms and together they cried for the mommy that was gone.

Then **suddenly** the little girl did something that the woman thought was a bit strange. She stopped crying, stepped back from the woman and began to sing. She sang so **softly** that it was almost a **whisper**. It was the sweetest sound the woman had ever heard, almost like the

"你喜欢我的连衣裙吗？"她问一位正走过她身边的陌生人。"

"我妈妈专给我做的。"她说道，眼里冒出了泪珠。

"嗯，我认为你的裙子真漂亮。告诉我，小姑娘，你为什么哭呢？"

小姑娘声音有些颤抖，回答道："我妈妈给我做完这条裙子后就不得不离开了。"

"哦，是这样，"陌生的女士说，"有你这样一个小姑娘等着她，我敢肯定她很快就会回来的。"

"不，女士，您不明白，"女孩透过泪水说，"我爸说她现在和我爷爷在天堂里。"

女士终于明白孩子的意思了，也明白她为什么哭泣。她跪下，温柔地把女孩搂在怀里，她们一起为离去的妈妈哭泣。

小姑娘忽然又做了件让女士感到有点奇怪的事。她停住了哭泣，从女士怀抱中抽出身，向后退了一步，然后开始唱歌。她唱得如此轻柔，几乎像低语。这是女士听到过的最

song of a very small bird.

After the child stopped singing she explained to the lady, "My mommy used to sing that song to me before she went away, and she made me promise to sing it whenever I started crying and it would make me stop."

"See," she **exclaimed**, "It did, and now my eyes are dry!"

As the woman turned to go, the little girl grabbed her sleeve, "Ma'am, can you stay just a minute? I want to show you something."

"Of course," she answered, "What do you want me to see?"

Pointing to a spot on her dress, she said, "Right here is where my mommy kissed my dress, and here," Pointing to another spot, "And here is another kiss, and here, and here. Mommy said that she put all those kisses on my dress so that I would have her kisses for every booboo' that made me cry."

Then the lady realized that she wasn't just looking at a dress, no, she was looking at a mother…who knew that she was going away and would not be there to kiss away the hurts that she knew her daughter would get.

So she took all the love she had for her beautiful little girl and put them into this dress, which her child now so

甜美的声音，简直就像一只非常小的鸟儿在吟唱。

小女孩唱完后解释说："妈妈离去前经常给我唱这支歌，她让我答应她我一哭就唱这支歌，这样我就不哭了。"

"您瞧，"她惊叫道，"真管用，现在我的眼睛里没有眼泪了！"

女士转身要走时，小女孩抓住她的衣袖："女士，您能再停留一小会儿吗？我想给您看点东西。"

"当然可以，"她回答，"你想要我看什么呢？"

小女孩指着裙子上的一处，说："就在这里，我妈妈亲了我的裙子，还有这里，"她指着另外一处，"这里有另外一个吻，还有这里，这里。妈妈说她把所有这些吻都留在我的连衣裙上，这样我遇到什么事哭了，就会有她的亲吻。"

这时，女士意识到在她眼前的不是一件连衣裙，不是的，她在凝视一位母亲……这位母亲知道她将离去，无法随时守候在女儿身边，吻去她知道女儿必然会遇到的种种伤心事。

所以她将所有对她美丽女儿的爱倾注在这件连衣裙上。现在，女儿如此骄傲地穿在身上。

proudly wore.

  She no longer saw a little girl in a simple dress. She saw a child wrapped—in her mother's love.

她看到的不再是身穿一件简单的连衣裙的小女孩。她看到的是一个孩子——一个被妈妈的爱包裹着的孩子。

单词解析 Word Analysis

quiver ['kwɪvə(r)] *n.* 颤音

例 There was a slight quiver in his voice as he spoke.
他说话时声音有些颤抖。

kneel [niːl] *v.* 下跪

例 Other people were kneeling, but she just sat.
其他人跪着，而她只是坐着。

cradle ['kreɪdl] *v.* 轻抱着（或捧着）

例 He was sitting at the big table cradling a large bowl of milky coffee.
他坐在一张大桌子旁，手里捧着一大碗加了牛奶的咖啡。

suddenly ['sʌdənli] *adv.* 突然地

例 Her expression suddenly altered.
她的表情一下子变了。

softly ['sɒftli] *adv.* 软的

例 When it's dry, brush the hair using a soft, nylon baby brush.
当头发干后，用柔软的婴儿用尼龙发刷梳理头发。

whisper ['wɪspə(r)] *n.* 低语，耳语

例 Her voice had sunk to a whisper.
她的声音越来越小，几乎成了窃窃私语。

exclaim [ɪksˈkleɪm] *v.* 突然喊叫

例 He exclaims that it must be a typing error.
他惊呼道那一定是个打印错误。

proudly ['praʊdli] *adv.* 自豪地，傲慢地

例 She proudly displayed her degree certificate to her parents.
她自豪地向父母展示了学位证书。

语法知识点 Grammar Points

① My mommy used to sing that song to me before she went away.

used to 意思是"过去经常"，其中to是不定式符号，不是介词，所以其后接动词原形。

例 He used to live in Paris.
他过去一直住在巴黎。
I used to write poetry when I was young.
我年轻时常常写诗。

used to 作为情态动词，可直接在used后加not构成否定式，直接将used置于句首构成疑问式，但与一般的情态动词不同，它也可像普通动词那样借助助动词did构成否定式和疑问式。

例 You used to go there, didn't you?
过去常到那儿去，是吗？

used to 与 often, always, never 等副词连用时，通常置于副词之后，也可置于副词之前。

例 I always used [used always] to be afraid of dogs.
我过去老是怕狗。
He often used [used often] to sit outside the door of his house.
他过去常坐他家门口。

② As the woman turned to go, the little girl grabbed her sleeve…

接动词的情况，turn to作"变成""转向（原来在做另外一件事）"。

例 He turned to keep silent when he saw me.
他看到我就安静了下来。

接名词的情况较为常见，"求助于，致力于"。

例 The child turned to his mother for comfort.
孩子向母亲寻求安慰。
The more depressed he got, the more he turned to drink.
他越郁闷就越喝酒消愁。

经典名句 *Famous Classics*

1. Failure is due to neglecting the details, and success begins with the emphasis on small things.
   失败缘于忽视细处，成功始于重视小事。

2. The brave and the wise can both pity and excuse, when cowards and fools show no mercy.
   勇者和智者均有同情谅解之心，而懦夫和愚者则毫无怜悯之心。

3. Calamity and prosperity are the touchstones of integrity.
   不幸与幸运都是正直的试金石。

读书笔记

21 The Key of a Car
一把车钥匙

A young man was getting ready to graduate from college. For many months he had admired a beautiful sports car in a dealer's showroom, and knowing his father could well **afford** it, he told him that was all he wanted.

As Graduation Day **approached**, the young man awaited signs that his father had purchased the car. Finally, on the morning of his graduation, his father called him into his private study. His father told him how proud he was to have such a fine son, and told him how much he loved him. He handed his son a beautiful wrapped gift box. **Curiously**, but somewhat disappointed, the young man opened the box and found a lovely, leather-bound *Bible*, with the young man's name embossed in gold. Angrily, he raised his voice to his father and said, "With all your money you give me a *Bible*?" Then he stormed out of the house, leaving the *Bible*.

Many years passed and the young man was very successful in business. He had a beautiful home and a wonderful family, but realizing his father was very

从前，有位年轻人即将大学毕业。数月来，他一直渴望得到某汽车商产品陈列室中的一辆跑车。他知道，他那富有的父亲肯定买得起这辆车，于是，他便跟父亲说他很想得到那辆漂亮的跑车。

在毕业典礼即将来临的日子里，年轻人等待着父亲买下跑车的消息。终于，在毕业典礼那天上午，父亲将他叫到自己的书房，并告诉他，有他这么出色的儿子自己感到非常自豪而且非常爱他这个儿子。接着，父亲递给儿子一个包装精美的礼品盒。年轻人感到好奇，但带着些许失望地打开礼品盒，却发现里面是一本精美的精装本《圣经》，上面以金子凸印着年轻人的名字。看罢，年轻人怒气冲冲地向父亲大喊道："你有那么多钱，却只给我一本《圣经》？"说完，便丢下《圣经》，愤怒地冲出房子。

多年以后，年轻人已事业有成。他拥有一所漂亮的房

old, he thought perhaps he should go to see him. He had not seen him since that graduation day. Before he could make the arrangements, he received a **telegram** telling him his father had passed away, and willed all of his **possessions** to his son. He needed to come home immediately and take care of things.

When he arrived at his father's house, sudden **sadness** and regret filled his heart. He began to search through his father's important papers and saw the still new *Bible*, just as he had left it years ago. With tears, he opened the *Bible* and began to turn the pages. As he was reading, a car key dropped from the back of the Bible. It had a tag with the dealer's name, the same dealer who had the sports car he had desired. On the tag was the date of his **graduation**, and the words... "PAID IN FULL".

How many times do we miss blessings because they are not packaged as we expected? I trust you enjoyed this. Do not spoil what you have by desiring what you have not; but remember that what you now have was once among the things you only hoped for.

Sometimes we don't realize the good **fortune** we have or we could have because we expect "the packaging" to be different. What may appear as bad

子，一个温馨的家庭。但当得知父亲年事已高，他想，或许应该去看看他。自从毕业那天起他就一直不见父亲。就在起程时，他收到一封电报——父亲已逝世，并已立下遗嘱将其所有财产转给儿子。他要立即回父亲家处理后事。

在父亲的房子里，他突然内心感到一阵悲伤与懊悔。他开始仔细搜寻父亲的重要文件，突然发现了那本《圣经》——还跟几年前一样崭新。他噙着泪水打开《圣经》并一页一页地阅读着。忽然，从书的背面掉出一把钥匙。钥匙上挂着一个标签，上面写着一个汽车经销商的名字——正是他曾渴望的那辆跑车的经销商。标签上还有他的毕业日期及"款已付清"的字样。

我们多少次地与祝福擦肩而过，仅仅因为他们没有按我们想象中的样子包装好？我相信你也有这样的经历。不要在渴望得到没有的东西时损坏你已经拥有的东西，但要记住一点：你现在所拥有的恰恰正是你曾经一心渴望得到的。

有时，我们并没有意识到我们已经拥有或本该拥有的好运，仅仅因为它的外表与我们想象中的有所不同。其实，表面上看起

fortune may in fact be the door that is just waiting to be opened.

来像是坏运气的东西或许正是等待开启的幸运之门。

单词解析 Word Analysis

afford [ə'fɔːd] v. 买得起，负担得起
例 My parents can't even afford a new refrigerator.
我父母甚至买不起一台新冰箱。

approach [əp'rəʊtʃ] v. 接近，走近，靠近
例 When I approached, they grew silent.
当我走近时，他们就不说话了。

curiously ['kjʊərɪəslɪ] adv. 好奇地，奇怪地
例 He's curiously innocent about what this means to other people.
关于这对其他人意味着什么，他一无所知，这一点颇不寻常。

telegram ['telɪgræm] n. 电报
例 Scores of congratulatory telegrams and letters greeted Franklin on his return.
富兰克林一回来，就收到了好几十封贺电和贺信。

possessions [pə'zeʃənz] n. 所有物；财产
例 People had lost their homes and all their possessions.
人们失去了自己的家园和所有的财物。

sadness ['sædnəs] n. 悲伤，忧愁，难过
例 He let out a long sigh, mainly of relief, partly of sadness.
他长叹一口气，主要是因为如释重负，也有一部分是因为伤心。

graduation [ˌgrædʒu'eɪʃn] n. 毕业；毕业典礼
例 They asked what his plans were after graduation.
他们问他毕业之后有何打算。

fortune ['fɔːtʃuːn] n. 财产，大笔的钱
例 Having spent his rich wife's fortune, the Major ended up in a

debtors' prison.
花光了他有钱老婆的财产之后，这位少校最后被关进了债务人监狱。

语法知识点 Grammar Points

① A young man was getting ready to graduate from college.

get ready to 准备做，为……做准备

例 You've got to keep your eyes open and mind sharp to get ready to jump at any chance.
还要睁大眼睛，保持头脑机敏，随时准备抓住任何机遇。

Wangjing is a transfer station. Passengers for line 14, please get ready to get off the train.
望京站是换乘车站，换乘地铁14号线的乘客，请在望京站下车。

graduate from 从……毕业，进步，进展

例 I will have learned English for 10 years by the time I graduate from university next year.
等我明年大学毕业时，我就学了10年英语了。

I will graduate from Beijing University with a master's degree in June of this year.
我将于今年6月毕业于北京大学，获得硕士学位。

graduate in 毕业于……学科

例 My son hopes to graduate in law, so as to become a lawyer.
我的儿子希望在大学攻读法律，毕业成为律师。

② He had not seen him since that graduation day.

since可做连词、副词和介词，本文中是作为连词，意思是"自从……以来〔以后或现在〕"，所表示的时间往往是从过去某一点时间一直延续到说话的时间，因而一般与完成时态连用。

例 He left the village in 1982 and I haven't seen him since then.
1982年他离开这个村子，从那以后我再没见过他。

since 作为介词，意思是"从……以来，自从……之后"，其宾语常指过去的一个时间点，其含意通常指持续到说话时刻的动作或情况开始于什么时候，之后常接名词、动名词作其宾语，since then意为"从那以后"。

The Key of a Car
一把车钥匙

例 Since then, he has developed another bad habit.
从那以后，他养成了另一种坏习惯。

He hasn't come close to those numbers since then.
自那以后，他从没有达到那赛季的表现。

since 用作副词表示"以前"时还可和 long，ever 连用。long since 意为"好久以前"，not long since 意为"就在不久前"，ever since 意为"从那时起，此后一直"。

例 We have lived in Shanghai ever since we came to China.
自从我们来到中国之后就一直住在上海。

③ Do not spoil what you have by desiring what you have not; but remember that what you now have was once among the things you only hoped for.

what you have 这个用法是以 what 为引导的从句充当宾语，这在英语中是非常常见的用法。

例 They have done what they can to help her.
他们已经尽力帮助了她。

what 在名词性从句当中可以充当主语、表语和宾语，根据不同的语境有以下几种不同的含义：

表示"……的东西或……事情"（what= the thing that）

例 He saves what he earns.
他赚多少，积蓄多少。

表示"……的人或……样子"

例 He is no longer what he was.
他已经不是以前的那个样子了。

表示"……的数量或……数目"（what=the amount that）

例 The number of the students in our school is ten times what it was before liberation.
现在我校学生的数量是解放前的10倍。

表示"……的地方"（what=the place that）

例 This is what they call Salt Lake City.
这就是他们称为盐湖城的地方。

经典名句 Famous Classics

1. No target for targeted people forever.
   没有目标的人永远为有目标的人去努力。

2. Life is not successful, success is temporary; to be successful, not successful is temporary.
   做人不成功，成功是暂时的；做人成功，不成功也是暂时的。

3. When regrets take the place of dreams a man is old.
   当后悔取代了梦想，一个人才算老了。

4. Would rather be laughed at that time, do not smile for a lifetime.
   宁可被人笑一时，不可被人笑一辈子。

5. Journey of a thousand miles begins with single step.
   千里之行，始于足下。

读书笔记

22　A Box Full of Kisses
装满吻的盒子

The story goes that some time ago, a man punished his 3-year-old daughter for wasting a roll of gold wrapping paper. Money was tight and he became **infuriated** when the child tried to **decorate** a box to put under the Christmas tree. **Nevertheless**, the little girl brought the gift to her father the next morning and said, "This is for you, Daddy."

The man was embarrassed by his earlier **overreaction**, but his anger **flared** again when he found out the box was empty. He yelled at her, stating, "Don't you know, when you give someone a present, there is supposed to be something inside?" The little girl looked up at him with tears in her eyes and cried, "Oh, Daddy, it's not empty at all. I blew kisses into the box. They're all for you, Daddy."

The father was crushed. He put his arms around his little girl, and he begged for her **forgiveness**. Only a short time later, an accident took the life of the child. It is also told that her father kept that gold box by his bed for many years and, whenever he was **discouraged**, he

有这样一个故事，爸爸因为三岁的女儿浪费了一卷金色的包装纸而惩罚了她。家里很缺钱，当孩子想要用包装纸装饰一个挂在圣诞树上的盒子时，爸爸生气了。然而，第二天早上小女孩把盒子作为礼物送给了爸爸，"这是给你的，爸爸。"

女儿的这个行为让爸爸感到尴尬。但是当他发现盒子是空的时候，他的怒火再一次燃烧了。他对女儿喊道，"难道你不知道给别人礼物的时候，里面应该放有东西吗？"女孩抬头看着父亲，眼里含着泪水，"爸爸，盒子不是空的。我把吻放在了盒子里，都是给你的，爸爸。"

爸爸感动极了，他搂住女儿，恳请她的原谅。之后不久，一场事故夺走了小女孩的生命。据说，父亲便将那个小金盒子放在床头，一直陪伴着他的余生。无论何时他感到气馁或者遇到难办的事情，他就会打开礼盒，取出一个假想的吻，记起漂亮女儿给予了自己

would take out an **imaginary** kiss and remember the love of the child who had put it there.

In a very real sense, each of us, as humans beings, has been given a gold container filled with unconditional love and kisses. from our children, family members, friends, and God. There is simply no other possession, anyone could hold, more **precious** than this.

特殊的爱。

从一个非常真实的意义上说,我们每个人都被赠予过一个无形的金色礼盒,那里面装满了来自子女、家人、朋友及上帝无条件的爱与吻。人们所能拥有的最珍贵的礼物莫过于此了。

单词解析 Word Analysis

infuriate [ɪnˈfjʊərɪeɪt] *v.* 使十分恼火;使大怒
例 The champion was infuriated by the decision.
冠军对这一决定十分恼火。

decorate [ˈdekəreɪt] *v.* 装饰;装点;点缀
例 Use shells to decorate boxes, trays, mirrors or even pots.
用贝壳来装点盒子、托盘、镜子甚至花盆。

nevertheless [ˌnevəðəˈles] *conj.* 然而,尽管如此
例 He nevertheless completed the film with breathtaking speed.
但他还是以惊人的速度拍完了这部电影。

overreaction [ˌəʊvərɪˈækʃn] *n.* 反应过度
例 The market appeared to overreact, but this is not the case.
市场反应看似过激,但实际并非如此。

flared [fleəd] *adj.* (裙子或裤子)喇叭形的,阔腿的
例 In the 1970s they all had flared trousers.
20世纪70年代的时候他们人人都有喇叭裤。

A Box Full of Kisses
装满吻的盒子 22

forgiveness [fəˈɡɪvnəs] *n.* 原谅，宽恕
- 例 I offered up a short prayer for forgiveness.
  我做了个简短的祷告，祈求宽恕。

discourage [dɪsˈkʌrɪdʒ] *v.* 使泄气；使灰心
- 例 It may be difficult to do at first. Don't let this discourage you.
  万事开头难，别因此而灰心。

imaginary [ɪˈmædʒɪnəri] *adj.* 想象中的；假想的；虚构的
- 例 Lots of children have imaginary friends.
  许多孩子都会凭空想象一些朋友。

unconditional [ˌʌnkənˈdɪʃənl] *adj.* 无条件的
- 例 Children need unconditional love.
  孩子们需要无条件的爱。

precious [ˈpreʃəs] *adj.* 珍贵的，宝贵的
- 例 After four months in foreign parts, every hour at home was precious.
  在国外待了4个月后，在家的每一刻都是宝贵的。

语法知识点 Grammar Points

① He yelled at her, stating, "Don't you know, when you give someone a present, there is supposed to be something inside?" The little girl looked up at him with tears in her eyes and cried.

yell at 对……吼叫
- 例 "Please don't yell at me." She began to sniffle.
  "请不要对我大喊大叫。"她啜泣起来。
  Because when you wake up late or forget something, or whatever, you always yell at me.
  因为当你起床晚了或忘记什么东西，不管什么，你总是冲我大呼小叫。

stating... 现在分词做伴随状语。
- 例 He has been courting the director, hoping to get the leading role in the play.

117

他一直在讨好导演，想在剧中扮演主角。

伴随状语是指状语的动作伴随主句发生，它的特点是：它所表达的动作或状态是伴随着句子谓语动词的动作而发生或存在的。伴随状语的逻辑主语一般情况下必须是全句的主语，伴随状语与谓语动词所表示的动作或状态是同时发生的。

上文中是用动词的现在分词做伴随状语是其中一种形式，另外还有with结构、独立主格结构、形容词等可做伴随状语。

> The little girls were playing with snow with their hands frozen red.
>
> 小女孩们在玩雪，手都冻红了。
>
> The little boy goes to school, the little dog accompanying him every day.
>
> 这小孩每天去上学，那条小狗陪伴着他。
>
> Confident of the victory the players are fighting hard.
>
> 运动员们对比赛夺胜满怀信心，奋力拼搏。

② **In a very real sense, each one of us, as humans beings, have been given a gold container filled with unconditional love and kisses... from our children, family members, friends, and God.**

filled with 装满，充满，在文中为动词的过去分词短语做后置定语。

> The media have been filled with tales of horror and loss resulting from earthquake.
>
> 媒体上尽是地震所带来的恐惧和损失的报道。

过去分词短语做后置定语比较好掌握，也就是过去分词带有自己的副词或介词构成短语，少数时候带有逻辑主语的主语补足语。

> This is the castle captured by the British.
>
> 这是被英国人占领的城堡。

单个过去分词一般只能做前置定语，很少做后置定语，但是某些单个过去分词可以做后置定语。

> The boats used are beautifully painted and decorated with flowers of all colors.
>
> 所使用的船漆得很漂亮而且被各种颜色的花所装饰。
>
> This is the only machine required.
>
> 这是唯一需要的机器。

A Box Full of Kisses
装满吻的盒子

经典名句 *Famous Classics*

1. Difficult circumstances serve as a textbook of life for people.
   困难坎坷是人们的生活教科书。

2. Better to forgive others; don't let others forgive you.
   宁可自己去原谅别人，莫让别人来原谅你。

3. If you are not often encountered setbacks, this suggests that's not very innovative.
   如果你不是经常遇到挫折，这表明诺做的事情没有很大的创新性。

4. If you are doing your best, you will not have to worry about failure.
   如果你竭尽全力，你就不用担心失败。

5. The one living in other people's applause, is the person who cannot afford the test.
   活在别人的掌声中，是禁不起考验的人。

6. The man who has made up his mind to win will never say "impossible".
   凡是决心取得胜利的人是从来不说"不可能的"。

读书笔记

23 Not Just a Mom
母亲的含义

A woman named Emily renewing her driver's license at the county clerk's office was asked by the woman recorder to state her **occupation.** She hesitated, uncertain how to **classify** herself. "What I mean is," explained the recorder, "Do you have a job, or are you just a..."

"Of course I have a job," snapped Emily. "I'm a mother."

"We don't list 'mother' as an occupation... 'housewife' covers it," said the recorder **emphatically**.

I forgot all about her story until one day I found myself in the same situation. This time at our own town hall, the clerk was obviously a career woman, poised, **efficient,** and possessed of a high sounding title like, "official **interrogator**" or "town registrar." "What is your occupation?" she probed.

What made me say it, I do not know... the words simply popped out. "I'm a research associate in the field of child development and human relations."

The clerk paused, ballpoint pen frozen in midair, and looked up as though she had not heard right.

一位名叫埃米莉的妇女在县办事处给驾驶执照续期时，一名女记录员问及她的职业。她犹豫了一下，不敢肯定应如何将自己归类。"我意思是说你有没有工作，"那名记录员解释说，"还是说你只不过是一名……"

"我当然有工作，"埃米莉马上回答，"我是一名母亲。"

"我们这里不把'母亲'看成是一个职业……'家庭主妇'就可以了。"那名记录员断然回答。

这个故事听后，我就忘了。直到有一天在市政厅，我也遇到了同样的情况。很显然，那名办事员是位职业女性，自信、有能力，并有着一个类似"官方讯问员"或"镇登记员"之类很堂皇的头衔。"你的职业？"她问道。

至今我也不知道，当时是什么因素作怪，我脱口而出："我是儿童发育和人类关系研究员。"

那名办事员愣住了，拿着圆珠笔的手也不动了。她抬头

Not Just a Mom
母亲的含义

I repeated the title slowly, emphasizing the most **significant** words. Then I stared with wonder as my pronouncement was written in bold, black ink on the official **questionnaire**.

"Might I ask," said the clerk with new interest, "Just what you do in your field?"

Coolly, without any trace of **fluster** in my voice, I heard myself reply, "I have a continuing program of research, (what mother doesn't), in the laboratory and in the field, (normally I would have said indoors and out). I'm working for my masters, (the whole darned family) and already have four credits, (all daughters). Of course, the job is one of the most demanding in the humanities, (any mother care to disagree?) and I often work 14 hours a day, (24 is more like it). But the job is more challenging than most run-of-the-mill careers and the rewards are more of a satisfaction rather than just money."

Motherhood—what a glorious career! Especially when there's a title on the door!

看着我，好像没有听清楚我说什么似的。

我慢慢把我的职业再重复一遍，在说到重要的词时还加重语气。然后，我惊奇地看着我的话被粗黑的笔记录在官方的问卷上。

"我能不能问一下，"这名办事员好奇地问，"你在这个领域具体做什么？"

我非常镇定地答道："我有一个不间断的研究项目（哪位母亲不是这样呢？），工作地点包括实验室和现场（通常我会说室内和户外），我在为我的学位努力（就是我们一家人），而且已经有了四个学分（全部是女儿）。当然，我的工作是人类要求最高的工作之一（有哪位母亲会反对吗？），我通常工作一天14小时（24小时更为准确）。但这项工作比大部分普通工作都具有挑战性，而它通常带来的回报不是金钱，更多的是满足感。"

母亲——这是多么光荣的职业啊！特别是现在这已经成为官方记录了。

单词解析 Word Analysis

occupation [ˌɒkjuˈpeɪʃn] *n.* 职业

例 I suppose I was looking for an occupation which was going to be

an adventure.
我想我在找的是一份具有冒险性的工作。

classify [ˈklæsɪfaɪ] *v.* 把……分类，为……归类
例 It is necessary initially to classify the headaches into certain types.
首先，必须将头痛分为几个类型。

emphatically [ɪmˈfætɪklɪ] *adv.* 强调地，加强语气地，断然地
例 Mr. Davies has emphatically denied the charges.
戴维斯先生断然否认了那些控诉。

efficient [ɪˈfɪʃnt] *adj.* 效率高的，效能高的
例 With today's more efficient contraception women can plan their families and careers.
如今有了更加有效的避孕方法，女性便可以规划她们的家庭和事业。

interrogator [ɪnˈterəgeɪtə(r)] *n.* 讯问者，审问者
例 Miss Fan lacked such an interrogator with whom she could whisper intimately.
范小姐就缺少这样一个窃窃私语的盘问者。

significant [sɪgˈnɪfɪkənt] *adj.* 重要的，有意义的
例 Time would appear to be the significant factor in this whole drama.
时间似乎是整部剧中一个举足轻重的因素。

questionnaire [ˌkwestʃəˈneə(r)] *n.* 调查表，调查问卷
例 Head teachers will be asked to fill in a questionnaire.
校长们将被要求完成一份问卷调查。

fluster [ˈflʌstə(r)] *n.* 慌乱；狼狈；混乱
例 She was put in a fluster by the unexpected guests.
不速之客的到来弄得她很慌张。

Not Just a Mom
母亲的含义

语法知识点 *Grammar Points*

① **The clerk paused, ballpoint pen frozen in midair, and looked up as though she had not heard right.**

as though 好像，仿佛

- I felt as though I should mention it as an option.
  我觉得我好像应该把它作为一种选择提出来。

英语中还有另外一个意思相同的词组as if，二者没有区别，as if用得普遍些，都可以引导方式状语从句和表语从句，其从句谓语常用虚拟语气。

- She acted as though nothing had happened.
  她装得好像什么事也没发生过似的。

当从句主语和主句主语一致，从句谓语中又含有动词to be时，可以把主语和to be一起省略。

- He paused as if (he was) expecting Tom to speak.
  他停了下来，好像期望汤姆说些什么。

as though和as if 从句用虚拟语气还是陈述语气，要根据具体情况而定。如果从句表示的意思与事实相反，或者纯粹是一种假设，通常用虚拟语气。

- When a pencil is partly in a glass of water, it looks as if it were broken.
  当铅笔的一部分放进水里，看起来好像是折断了似的。（虚拟）

② **But the job is more challenging than most run-of-the-mill careers and the rewards are more of a satisfaction rather than just money.**

more challenging 更具挑战性，challenging是多音节形容词，构成比较级在前面加more。

- I resigned from the foreign company in order to take a more challenging job.
  为了能够接受一个更具有挑战性的工作，我从外企辞职了。

more of a/an + n...指数量或程度上更"更（像/是）……"，表示更具有某种特质，相当于more like a(n)...，常作宾语或表语。

- No, I wouldn't call it maroon. I'd say it's more of a burgundy.
  不，我觉得不是褐红色，更像是酒红色。

I'd say travelling during Spring Festival is more of a battle than a vacation.

我觉得春节期间的旅行更像是一场战斗，而不是假期。

rather than（要）……而不……，与其……倒不如，可做连词，可做介词，than后直接加动词原形，而不是不定式to do。

例 Vector graphics are a complement, rather than an alternative, to bitmap graphics.

对于位图来说，矢量图像是一种补充，而不是替代。

I prefer to work rather than remain idle.

比起无所事事，我更喜欢工作。

经典名句 Famous Classics

1. Waterfall in order to run into rivers and lakes, even facing a hundred feet deep, still roaring forward, never retreat.
   瀑布为了奔向江河湖海，即使面临百丈深渊，仍然呼啸前行，决不退缩。

2. Lonely people always remember the life of every man, as I kept thinking of you!
   寂寞的人总是记住生命中出现的每一个人，正如我总是意犹未尽地想起你！

3. Sometimes, no matter how hard you try, he will leave you and be replaced by a better person.
   有时候，不管你如何努力，他总会离你而去，然后被一个更好的人所代替。

4. We can't waste time; we just waste ourselves.
   我们无法浪费时间，我们浪费的只是我们自己。

5. Know yourselves, yield yourselves, change yourselves to change others.
   认识自己，降伏自己，改变自己，才能改变别人。

24 All You Remember
你所记得的一切

All you remember about your child being an infant is the **incredible** awe you felt about the **precious** miracle you created. You remember having plenty of time to bestow all your wisdom and knowledge. You thought your child would take all of your advice and make fewer mistakes, and be much smarter than you were. You wished for your child to hurry and grow up.

All you remember about your child being two is never using the restroom alone or getting to watch a movie without talking animals. You recall afternoons talking on the phone while **crouching** in the bedroom closet, and being convinced your child would be the first ivy league college student to graduate wearing **pullovers** at the ceremony. You remember worrying about the bag of m&m's melting in your pocket and ruining your good dress. You wished for your child to be more independent.

All you remember about your child being seven is the carpool schedule. You learned to apply makeup in two minutes and brush your teeth in the **rearview**

当你的孩子是个婴儿时，你所记得的，是你对自己创造出的堪称完美奇迹的作品，感到不可思议的敬畏。你记得你有大量的时间去传授你所有的智慧和知识。你认为你的孩子将会接受你所有的忠告而少犯错误，将会比孩提时代的你聪明许多。你多希望你的孩子快快长大。

孩子两岁时，你所记得的，是从不能独自使用卫生间，从不看一部与动物无关的电影。你记得那些蜷缩在卧室储衣间跟朋友通电话的下午，深信你的孩子将是第一个身着套头衫出席毕业典礼的常春藤名牌大学毕业生。你记得你担心那袋m&m巧克力糖会在你的衣兜里融化，毁了你体面的衣服。你多希望你的孩子更独立些。

孩子7岁时，你所记得的，是合伙用车的时间安排。你学会了在两分钟内化完妆，照着汽车后视镜刷牙，因为你能给你自己找出的时间就只有汽车停在红灯前的那一小段。

mirror because the only time you had to yourself was when you were stopped at red lights. You considered painting your car yellow and posting a "taxi" sign on the lawn next to the garage door. You remember people staring at you, the few times you were out of the car, because you kept flexing your foot and making **acceleration** noises. You wished for the day your child would learn how to drive.

All you remember about your child being ten is managing the school fund raisers. You sold wrapping paper for paint, T-shirts for new furniture, and magazine **subscriptions** for shade trees in the school playground. You remember storing a hundred cases of candy bars in the garage to sell so the school band could get new uniforms, and how they melted together on an **unseasonably** warm spring afternoon. You wished your child would grow out of playing an instrument.

All you remember about your child being sixteen is loud music and **undecipherable** lyrics screamed to a **rhythmic** beat. You wished for your child to grow up and leave home with the stereo.

All you remember about your child being eighteen is the day they were born and having all the time in the world.

你想过把你的车子漆成黄色，并在车库门旁的草坪上立一个"出租车"的标志牌。你记得有几次你下车后，人们盯着你，因为你不断用脚踩油门加速、制造噪声。你多希望孩子有一天能学会开车。

孩子10岁时，你所记得的，是怎么组织学校的募捐者。你们为重新粉刷学校兜售包装纸，为购置新家具兜售T恤衫，为在学校操场上种植遮阳树劝人订阅各种杂志。你记得你在车库里存放了上百盒糖果等待出售，得到钱后学校的乐队就可以购置新制服，可是那些糖果竟在一个暖和得过头的春天下午全都融化在一起了。你多希望孩子长大，不再演奏什么乐器了。

孩子16岁时，你所记得的，是吵闹的音乐和以富有节奏的拍子尖声唱出的难以听懂的歌词。你多希望孩子快点长大成人，带着音响离开家吧。

孩子18岁时，你所记得的，是他们出生的那一天，拥有世间所有的时光。

当你在静静的房子里走来走去时，你纳闷他们去哪里了，你多希望孩子别这么快就长大了。

And, as you walk through your quiet house, you wonder where they went and you wish your child hadn't grown up so fast.

单词解析 Word Analysis

incredible [ɪnˈkredəbl] *adj.* 不可思议的，难以置信的

例 We should not dismiss as lies the incredible stories that children may tell us.
我们不应把孩子们告诉我们的一些不可思议的故事当成谎话而不予理睬。

precious [ˈpreʃəs] *adj.* 珍贵的，宝贵的

例 A family break allows you to spend precious time together.
家庭度假会让你们一起度过宝贵的时光。

crouch [ˈkraʊtʃ] *v.* 屈膝，蹲伏

例 We were crouching in the bushes.
我们蹲在树丛里。

pullover [ˈpʊlˌəʊvə] *n.* 套头毛衣

例 Pullovers can be left off in this warm weather.
天气这么暖和，可以不穿套头毛衣了。

rearview [ˈrɪəvjuː] *n.* 后视镜

例 Always focus on the front windshield and not the rearview mirror.
专心看车前的挡风玻璃，别看后视镜。

acceleration [əkˌseləˈreɪʃn] *n.* 加速

例 He has also called for an acceleration of political reforms.
他同时呼吁加快政治改革的步伐。

subscription [səbˈskrɪpʃn] *n.* （报刊等的）订阅费

例 You can become a member by paying the yearly subscription.

支付一年的会员费就可以成为会员。

unseasonably [ʌnˈsiːznəbli] *adv.* 反季节地，不合时宜地

例 It was unseasonably mild for late January.
一月下旬天气就这么暖和有点反常。

undecipherable [ˈʌndɪˈsaɪfərəbl] *adj.* 破译不出的，难辨认的

例 A hopelessly undecipherable jumble of overlapping names
一大团无法分辨、层层叠叠的名字

rhythmic [ˈrɪðmɪk] *adj.* 有韵律的，有节奏的

例 Good breathing is slow, rhythmic and deep.
健康的呼吸方式缓慢深沉而有节奏。

语法知识点 *Grammar Points*

① You remember having plenty of time to bestow all your wisdom and knowledge.

remember doing sth. 记得做过……（已做过）
remember to do sth. 记住去做……（还没做）

例 The biggest challenge for smiling is to remember to do it.
最大的挑战是记得去微笑。
Don't you remember telling me the story yesterday?
难道你不记得昨天跟我讲过这个故事了吗？

类似的用法：
forget doing sth. 忘记做过……（已做）
forget to do sth. 忘记该做……（还未做）
stop doing sth. 停止做……（同一件）
stop to do sth. 停下来去做……（另一件）

② All you remember about your child being two is never using the restroom alone or getting to watch a movie without talking animals.

alone 独自，单独

All You Remember 你所记得的一切 24

例 There is nothing so fearful as to be alone in a combat situation.
没有比孤身奋战更可怕的了。

容易和lonely混淆用法：
alone既可以作形容词，也可以用作副词。而lonely只能用作形容词；alone经常放在名词或者代词后面，作为后置定语。而lonely通常放在名词或代词前面，作前置定语，并且lonely有时还可以作表语；alone多指处于一个人的状态，含有享受孤寂、孤单的意思，没有太强的感情色彩。而lonely更强调一种孤独感，希望能有人陪伴、消除寂寞的感情色彩。

例 I don't like being alone; it makes me feel lonely.
我不喜欢一个人，那会让我感到很孤独。

Normally, a lonely person is introverted.
孤独的人通常性格比较内向。

③ **You wished your child would grow out of playing an instrument.**

grow out of 产生自……；从……发展；渐渐穿不上；停止

例 Most children who stammer grow out of it.
大多数口吃的儿童长大以后就好了。

You've grown out of your shoes again.
你又长大了，原来的鞋子再也穿不下了。

常用短语：
grow out of date 变得过时
grow out of knowledge 忘记
grow out of shoes 鞋穿小了
grow out of a habit 戒除一个习惯

经典名句 Famous Classics

1. If you have to lose, I hope that is sadness! If you must forget, I wish that is trouble!
   如果必须失去，但愿是忧愁！如果必须遗忘，但愿是烦恼！

2. Dream is a beautiful journey; before everyone finds it, he is just a lonely boy.
   梦想是一场华美的旅途，每个人在找到它之前，都只是孤独的少年。

3. Success without happiness is the biggest failure.
成功了而没有快乐,是最大的失败。

4. Life is like a buffet.
人生就像自助餐。

读书笔记

25 Brother's Wish
哥哥的心愿

A friend of mine named Paul received an **automobile** from his brother as a Christmas present. On Christmas Eve when Paul came out of his office, a street **urchin** was walking around the **shiny** new car, admiring it.

"Is this your car, Mister?" he said.

Paul nodded. "My brother gave it to me for Christmas." The boy was astounded. "You mean your brother gave it to you and it didn't cost you anything? Boy, I wish..." He hesitated.

Of course Paul knew what he was going to wish for. He was going to wish he had a brother like that. But what the lad said **jarred** Paul all the way down to his heels.

"I wish," the boy went on, "That I could be a brother like that."

Paul looked at the boy in **astonishment**, then **impulsively** he added, "Would you like to take a ride in my car?"

"Oh yes, I'd love that."

After a short ride, the boy turned with his eyes **aglow**, said, "Mister, would you mind driving in front of my house?"

Paul smiled a little. He thought he

我有一位朋友叫保罗,他在圣诞节收到了哥哥送来的一辆轿车。圣诞节前夕,保罗走出办公室时,一个乞丐绕着他那闪亮的新车,满口称赞。

"先生,这是你的车吗?"他问道。

保罗点了下头。"这是我哥哥送给我的圣诞礼物。"男孩震惊了。"你是说你的哥哥把它送给你了,而你一分钱也没花?天啊!我希望……"他顿了顿。

保罗当然知道男孩希望什么。他希望自己能有一个那样的哥哥。但少年接下来的话让保罗猝不及防。

"我希望,"男孩接着说,"希望我能成为那样的哥哥。"

保罗惊讶地看着男孩,情不自禁地说:"你想不想坐着我的车去兜兜风?"

"哦,太棒了!我太愿意了。"

驶出一小段路后,男孩转过头,双眼闪着光芒,说:"先生,你可不可以让车经过

knew what the lad wanted. He wanted to show his neighbors that he could ride home in a big automobile. But Paul was wrong again. "Will you stop where those two steps are?" the boy asked.

He ran up the steps. Then in a little while Paul heard him coming back, but he was not coming fast. He was carrying his little **crippled** brother. He sat him down on the bottom step, then sort of squeezed up against him and pointed to the car.

"There she is, Buddy, just like I told you upstairs. His brother gave it to him for Christmas and it didn't cost him a cent. And some day I am gonna give you one just like it... then you can see for yourself all the pretty things in the Christmas windows that I've been trying to tell you about."

Paul got out and lifted the lad to the front seat of his car. The shining-eyed older brother climbed in beside him and the three of us began a **memorable** holiday ride.

That Christmas Eve, Paul learned what Jesus meant when he said, "It is more blessed to give than to receive."

我的房前？"

保罗微微笑了下。他觉得自己知道男孩想要做什么。他要向邻居们炫耀他是坐着一辆大轿车回家的。但保罗又猜错了。"你可不可以在两个台阶那里停车？"男孩问道。

男孩冲上台阶。不一小会儿，保罗就听到了他返回的脚步声，但是动作并不快。男孩带着他跛足的弟弟出来了。他让弟弟坐在第一个台阶上，紧紧抱住他，指着那辆车。

"弟弟，看啊，这就是我在楼上和你说的那辆车。那是他哥哥送给他的圣诞礼物，而他自己一分钱也没花。总有一天，我也要送你一份那样的礼物……然后你就能亲眼看看圣诞橱窗里，那些我一直试着向你描述的美丽饰物。"

保罗走下车，把弟弟放在前座上。哥哥双眼闪着光，爬进车坐在弟弟身旁，就这样我们三个开启了一段难忘的假日旅程。

在那个平安夜，保罗理解了耶稣所说的话——施舍比收受更有福气。

Brother's Wish 哥哥的心愿

单词解析 Word Analysis

automobile [ˈɔːtəməbiːl] *n.* 汽车

例 My father had a narrow squeak in the automobile accident.
我父亲在这次车祸中死里逃生。

urchin [ˈɜːtʃɪn] *n.* 肮脏而衣着破烂的儿童

例 We were in the bazaar with all the little urchins watching us.
我们在集市里，周围一大帮衣衫褴褛的小孩盯着我们看。

shiny [ˈʃaɪnɪ] *adj.* 闪亮的，反光的，有光泽的

例 Her blonde hair was shiny and clean.
她的金发干净而有光泽。

jar [dʒɑː(r)] *v.* 令人不快；使人不安

例 Sometimes a light remark jarred on her father.
有时候一句玩笑就会令她父亲不快。

astonishment [əˈstɒnɪʃmənt] *n.* 惊讶，惊奇，令人诧异的事物

例 I spotted a shooting star which, to my astonishment, was bright green in color.
我看见一颗流星，使我大为惊奇的是，它居然是鲜亮的绿色。

impulsively [ɪmˈpʌlsɪvlɪ] *adv.* 易冲动地，草率地

例 Impulsively she patted him on the arm.
她很冲动地拍了拍他的胳膊。

aglow [əˈgləʊ] *adv.* 面色发红地，满面红光地

例 "It was incredible," Kurt says, suddenly aglow.
"简直难以置信，"库尔特突然满面红光地说。

crippled [ˈkrɪpld] *adj.* 残废的，跛腿的

例 Impulsively she patted him on the arm.
她很冲动地拍了拍他的胳膊。

memorable [ˈmemərəbl] *adj.* 难忘的，值得纪念的

例 Her speech was memorable for its polemic rather than its

substance.

她的演说之所以令人难忘，不是因其内容而是因其辩论方法。

语法知识点 Grammar Points

① You mean your brother gave it to you and it didn't cost you anything?

cost sb. sth. 花费某人……，可以是时间，也可以是金钱或精力，主语是物或某种活动。

sth. costs (sb.) +金钱，某物花了（某人）多少钱

例 A new computer costs a lot of money.
买一台新电脑要花一大笔钱。

(doing) sth. costs (sb.) +时间，某物（做某事）花了（某人）多少时间

例 Remembering these new words cost him a lot of time.
他花了大量时间才记住了这些单词。

cost的过去式及过去分词都是cost，并且不能用于被动句。
英语表示"花费"，常见的还有spend（前文中有介绍过）以及take。
take后面常跟双宾语，常见用法有以下几种：
It takes sb. +时间+to do sth. 做某事花了某人多少时间

例 It took them three years to build this road.
他们用了三年时间修完了这条路。

doing sth. takes sb. +时间，做某事花了某人多少时间

例 Repairing this car took him the whole afternoon.
他花了一下午修车。

② He ran up the steps. Then in a little while Paul heard him coming back, but he was not coming fast.

in a little while 不一会儿，不久

例 This was the pinnacle of my happiness, from which I was in a little while dashed to earth.
可以说，这把我推到了快乐的顶点，但是片刻之间，我就从云端直坠地面。

She is unconscious now, but may come to life in a little while.
她现在失去知觉了，但过一会儿可能会恢复知觉。

文中的 while 做名词，表"一段时间"，while 也可做连词，译为"虽然"，"与……同时"。

> **例** They were grinning and watching while one man laughed and poured beer over the head of another.
> 当一个男人大笑着把啤酒倒在另一个人头上时，他们都在乐呵呵地看着。
> There's plenty of rain in the southeast, while there's little in the northeast.
> 东南部雨量充足，而东北部则很少下雨。

经典名句 Famous Classics

1. To feel the flame of dreaming and to feel the moment of dancing; when all the romance is far away, the eternity is always there.
感受梦的火焰，感觉飞舞瞬间，当一切浪漫遥远，永恒依然。

2. A man has two ears and one mouth that he may hear much and speak little.
人有两只耳朵一张嘴，就是为了多听少说话。

3. We put down the dignity and the character because we cannot put down a person.
我们放下尊严，放下个性，都是因为放不下一个人。

4. Everyone makes mistakes; that's why eraser is put in the pencil.
每个人都会犯错，这就是为什么把橡皮擦安在铅笔后面的原因。

5. It is not easy to make friendship into love, and it is more difficult to turn love into friendship.
让友情变成爱情不是件容易的事，而让爱情变成友情更困难。

读书笔记

26 The Apple Tree
苹果树

A long time ago, there was a huge apple tree. A little boy loved to come and lay around it every day. He climbed to the tree top, ate the apples, took a nap under the **shadow**. He loved the tree and the tree loved to play with him.

Time went by, the little boy had grown up and he no longer played around the tree every day. One day, the boy came back to the tree and he looked sad. "Come and play with me," the tree asked the boy. "I am no longer a kid, I don't play around trees anymore." The boy replied, "I want toys. I need money to buy them." "Sorry, but I don't have money, but you can pick all my apples and sell them. So, you will have money." The boy was so **excited**. He grabbed all the apples on the tree and left happily. The boy never came back. The tree was so sad.

One day, the boy returned and the tree was so excited. "Come and play with me," the tree said. " I don't have time to play. I have to work for my family. We need a house for **shelter**. Can you help me?" "Sorry, but I don't have a house. But you can chop off my

很久以前，有一棵又高又大的苹果树。一位小男孩，天天到树下，他爬上去摘苹果吃，在树荫下睡觉。他爱苹果树，苹果树也爱和他一起玩耍。

后来，小男孩长大了，不再天天来玩耍。一天他又来到树下，很伤心的样子，苹果树要和他一起玩，男孩说："不行，我不小了，不能再和你玩了，我要玩具，可是没钱买。"苹果树说："很遗憾，我也没钱，不过，把我所有的果子摘下来卖掉，你不就有钱了？"男孩十分激动，他摘下所有的苹果，高高兴兴地走了。男孩好久都没有来，苹果树很伤心。

有一天，男孩终于来了，树兴奋地邀他一起玩。男孩说："不行，我没有时间，我要替家里干活呢，我们需要一幢房子，你能帮忙吗？""我没有房子，"苹果树说，"不过你

The Apple Tree
苹果树

branches to build your house." So the boy cut all the **branches** off the tree and left happily. The tree was glad to see him happy but the boy never came back since then. The tree was again lonely and sad.

One hot summer day, the boy returned and the tree was **delighted**. "Come and play with me!" The tree said. " I am sad and getting old. I want to go sailing to relax myself. Can you give me a boat?" "Use my **trunk** to build your boat. You can sail far away and be happy." So the boy cut the tree trunk to make a boat. He went sailing and never showed up for a long time. The tree was happy, but it was not true.

Finally, the boy returned after he left for so many years. "Sorry, my boy, but I don't have anything for you anymore, no more apples for you." the tree said.

This is a story of everyone. The tree is our parent. When we were young, we loved to play with mom and dad... when we grew up, we left them, and only came to them when we needed something or when we were in trouble. No matter what, parents would always be there and give everything they could to make you happy. You may think that the boy is **cruel** to the tree but that's how all of us are treating our parents.

可以把我的树枝统统砍下来，拿去搭房子。"于是男孩砍下所有的树枝，高高兴兴地运走去盖房子。看到男孩高兴，树好快乐。从此，男孩又不来了，树再次陷入孤单和悲伤之中。

一个炎热的夏日，男孩回来了，树太快乐了："来呀！孩子，来和我玩呀。"男孩却说："我心情不好，一天天老去，我要扬帆出海，轻松一下，你能给我一艘船吗？"苹果树说："把我的树干砍去，拿去做船吧！"于是男孩砍下了她的树干，造了条船，然后驾船走了，很久都没有回来。树好快乐，但不是真的。

许多年过去，男孩终于回来，苹果树说："对不起，孩子，我已经没有东西可以给你了，我没有苹果了。"

这就是我们每个人的故事。这棵树就是我们的父母，小时候，我们喜欢和爸爸妈妈玩……长大后，我们就离开他们，只有在需要什么东西或者遇到麻烦的时候，才回到他们身边。无论如何，父母永远都在那儿，倾其所有使你快乐。你可能认为这个男孩对树很残酷，但这就是我们每个人对待父母的方式。

No matter how busy you are, share some time with parents.

不管你有多忙，都要花些时间陪陪自己的父母。

单词解析 Word Analysis

shadow ['ʃædəʊ] *n.* 影子

例 An oak tree cast its shadow over a tiny round pool.
一棵橡树的影子投射在一洼圆形的小水池上。

excited [ɪk'saɪtɪd] *adj.* 激动的，兴奋的

例 I was so excited when I went to sign the paperwork that I could hardly write.
去签文件时我非常兴奋，几乎无法写字。

shelter ['ʃeltə(r)] *n.* 遮蔽，庇护，掩蔽

例 The number of families seeking shelter rose by 17 percent.
寻求避难的家庭户增加了17%。

branch [brɑːntʃ] *n.* 树枝；（企业或组织的）分支机构，分部

例 The local branch of Bank of America is handling the accounts.
美国银行在当地的分行正在处理这些账目。

delighted [dɪ'laɪtɪd] *adj.* 高兴的，愉快的

例 He said that he was delighted with the public response.
他说公众的反应让他欣喜。

trunk [trʌŋk] *n.* 树干

例 There is a new trunk growing from the fallen dead tree.
从倒下的枯树上长出一棵新树干。

cruel [kruːəl] *adj.* 残忍的，残酷的

例 Don't you think it's cruel to cage a creature up?
你不认为把动物关进笼里太残忍了吗？

语法知识点 *Grammar Points*

① But you can chop off my branches to build your house.

chop off 砍掉，斩断

例 It can cleave cloud in the sky and chop off all obstacles.
上可以劈天上的浮云，下可以斩除地上所有的障碍。

chop away 洗刷

例 If only I could chop away the years. Shred the age from my mother's face and hands.
要是我能把这些年流逝的时间一扫而光就好了，将母亲脸上、手上的岁月沧桑抚平。

② …when we grew up, we left them, and only came to them when we needed something or when we were in trouble. No matter what, parents would always be there and give everything they could to make you happy.

in trouble 处于不幸中，惹麻烦

例 This is not the first time his exploits have landed him in trouble.
这已经不是他第一次因自己的冒险行为而惹上麻烦了。

People are saying if we don't buck up we'll be in trouble.
人们说，如果我们再不积极行动起来，我们就会有麻烦。

no matter what 无论什么，no matter+特殊疑问词相当于疑问词+ever后缀，类似还有no matter how 无论怎样，no matter which 无论哪个，no matter who 无论谁。

no matter常与疑问代词或疑问副词一起构成连词词组引导让步状语从句，意为"无论……"，由no matter what（who, where, when）引导的从句往往用一般现在时或一般过去时。

例 No matter who you are, you must obey the rules.
无论你是谁，都应该遵守规则。

注意被修饰的名词、形容词以及副词的位置，no matter what/whose/which 修饰名词时，该名词必须紧跟其后；no matter how修饰形容词或副词时，该形容词或副词也必须紧跟其后。

例 No matter how hard he works, he finds it difficult to make ends meet.
无论他多么努力工作，却总是入不敷出。

经典名句 *Famous Classics*

1. The only limit to our realization of tomorrow will be our doubts of today.
   实现明天理想的唯一障碍是今天的疑虑。

2. The so-called love is when you take away the feeling, the passion, the romance, and you still care for that person.
   所谓爱,就是当感觉、热情和浪漫统统拿掉之后,你仍然珍惜对方。

3. If you are ever in trouble, don't try to be brave, just run, just run away.
   你若遇上麻烦,不要逞强,你就跑,远远跑开。

4. All people want to be happy, and do not want to bear the pain, but if you are not under the light rain, how can you experience the rainbow?
   所有人都想得到幸福,不愿承担痛苦,但是不下点小雨,哪儿来的彩虹?

5. If the hateful defeat makes you have tasted the bitter fruit, friends, rising will let you taste the joy of life.
   如果可恨的挫折使你尝到苦果,朋友,奋起必将让你尝到人生的欢乐。

读书笔记

27 New Shoes
一双新鞋子

Anne is six years older than me. Growing up, we were very poor, and my mother worked evenings at a factory in a small mid-western town. Not seeing my mother much, Anne took over much of the maternal support, and she was awarded the authority to give me and my younger sister **permission** to do things. Actually, going to Anne was much better than going to a parent as she could award permission, but never had an **urge** to punish us when we broke the rules. Therefore, we were a bit more willing to **confess** our activities to Anne and sometimes benefited from her **sisterly** advice. During those **turbulent** teenage years, Anne was always there for me, not only as a big sister, but as a mother and my best friend.

When I was seventeen and had no money, I thought my only chance of going to college was if I could win a **scholarship**. I had an important interview for such an award. Anne at that time was struggling, surviving on a part-time job as she put herself through the local community college after serving in the army. I told her of

安妮比我大六岁。小时候，我们家很穷，妈妈每晚都要在一家位于中西部小镇的工厂里劳作。由于不常见到妈妈，安妮肩负起了很多妈妈的责任。她得到了母亲的授权，能决定我和妹妹们能做哪些事情。实际上，去找安妮比直接去找父母好太多了——因为她能答应我们的请求，我们违反规定了却又从不惩罚我们。因此，我们更愿意向安妮坦言自己的所作所为，有时还会得益于她那来自姐姐角度提出的建议。在躁动不安的青少年岁月里，安妮一直陪伴着我，她不仅仅是一位大姐姐，更是一位母亲、一位最好的朋友。

我十七岁那年，家里也没什么钱，我认为自己能上大学的唯一机会就是获得奖学金。为了得到这笔奖学金，我要参加一场重要的面试。当时安妮生活得很艰苦，服完兵役后她靠着兼职工作赚的钱勉强维持自己进入当地的社区大学。我告诉她面试的事情：通用汽

my interview, that General Motors was sending me a bus ticket, and I would get to visit the city for my scholarship interview. It would be the first time I ever saw a city. I was excited about the **adventure** and asked her advice on what to wear. I showed her my best **outfit** and how I planned to be careful about how I sat so that the hole in the bottom of my shoe would not be seen, but I wasn't sure what I would do if it rained. I showed her how I would stand with my arm slightly in front of me to hide the **blemish** from my factory—second pants from the farmers' market. My best blouse was a find at a yard sale, slightly faded but still pretty.

　　Anne suggested that we go shopping, and we took the bus to the JCPenney store. She took me to the shoe department, and we found a beautiful pair of leather shoes on sale. She told me to try them on, but I thought it was just for fun as neither of us had ever owned anything that expensive before. Sometimes we did go shopping together and tried on things just to see what they looked and felt like, but we never could afford to buy them. It was like playing dress-up. But this time was different. Anne handed me the boxed shoes and said, "Here, I'll buy these for you."

　　But ... was all I could say.

车公司给我寄了一张车票，我将去往城市参加奖学金面试。这将是我第一次去大城市。我非常期待这次的"探险"，征询她我应该穿什么。我向她展示了我最好的衣物，以及我要如何小心坐姿以防别人看到我鞋底的洞，不过要是下雨了我不知道该怎么办。我向她演示站立时怎样把手臂微微放在身前，来挡住我从农贸市场买回的次品裤子上的污渍。我最好的衬衫是从二手市场淘到的，虽略微褪色却还是好看的。

　　安妮提议去逛商场，我们就乘公交去了杰西潘尼百货商场。她带我来到售鞋处，我们发现了一双漂亮的皮鞋。安妮叫我穿上试试，我觉得那只是为了好玩，因为我们谁都从来没有拥有过如此昂贵的东西。有时，我们会一起逛街，试穿衣服，不过只是为了体验一下那些穿起来是什么样子、感觉如何，但我们从来都买不起。我们就像在玩变装游戏一样。但此时却不同了。安妮把包装好的鞋子递给我，说："给，这是我买给你的。"

　　"可……"这是我唯一能

New Shoes 一双新鞋子

"You **deserve** them," she replied. "This interview is important. I want to see you get that scholarship."

I was **speechless** as I knew this was a lot of money for her, and she would probably have to eat nothing but ramen noodles for at least a month.

I went to the interview and crossed my legs so that my beautiful new shoes shone with pride. I won the scholarship and became an engineer. Although they were nice leather everyday shoes, I didn't wear them much because they were so special. I hope Anne didn't think I did not like them or something. Now, after twenty years have passed, I still have that pair of shoes with me, and I just wear them on those little occasions when I need to feel special. It's kind of like having magic ruby slippers when you're **homesick**.

"你值得拥有这些,"她说,"这次面试很重要。我希望你获得奖学金。"

我说不出话了,因为我知道这对她来说是一大笔钱,而她极可能在至少一个月内都只能吃泡面。

我去参加了面试,骄傲地跷起二郎腿,我漂亮的新鞋闪着光芒。我拿到了奖学金,成了一名工程师。尽管它们是优质的皮鞋,适合日常穿着,但因为它们太特别了,我也就不怎么穿了。我希望安妮不会觉得我不喜欢它们或是怎样。如今,十二年已经过去了,那双鞋一直陪伴着我,而我只在特殊的场合才会穿上。就像当你想家时,会穿上那双有魔力的红舞鞋一样。

单词解析 Word Analysis

permission [pəˈmɪʃn] *n.* 准许,许可

例 He asked permission to leave the room.
他请求准许离开房间。

urge [ɜːdʒ] *n.* 强烈的欲望;冲动

例 He had an urge to open a shop of his own.
他很想自己开一家店。

confess [kənˈfes] *v.* 承认,供认,坦白(自己做错的事)

例 Her husband confessed to having had an affair.

她丈夫承认有过外遇。

sisterly ['sɪstəli] *adj.* 姐妹般的
例 We just had a sisterly relationship.
我们只是姐妹般的关系。

turbulent ['tɜːbjələnt] *adj.* 变幻莫测的；动荡的，骚乱的；混乱的
例 The turbulent world of Middle Eastern politics defies prediction.
中东动荡不安的政治局势让人难以预测。

scholarship ['skɒləʃɪp] *n.* 奖学金
例 He got a scholarship to the Pratt Institute of Art.
他获得了普拉特艺术学院的奖学金。

adventure [əd'ventʃə(r)] *n.* 冒险，奇遇；大胆的开拓
例 Their cultural backgrounds gave them a spirit of adventure.
他们的文化背景赋予了他们一种冒险精神。

outfit ['aʊtfɪt] *n.* 全套服装
例 I spent lots of money on smart new outfits for work.
我花大笔钱购置了上班时穿的漂亮新套装。

blemish ['blemɪʃ] *n.* 缺陷；不足
例 This is the one blemish on an otherwise resounding success.
如果没有这个小小的失误，这就是一次彻底的胜利。

deserve [dɪ'zɜːv] *v.* 应得；应受；值得
例 Government officials clearly deserve some of the blame as well.
政府官员显然也应当承担部分责任。

speechless ['spiːtʃləs] *adj.* （因惊愕）一时语塞的
例 Alex was almost speechless with rage and despair.
亚历克斯又生气又绝望，几乎说不出话来。

homesick ['həʊmsɪk] *adj.* 想家的
例 She's feeling a little homesick.
她有点想家。

New Shoes 一双新鞋子 27

语法知识点 Grammar Points

① **Anne at that time was struggling, surviving on a part-time job as she put herself through the local community college after serving in the army.**

put through 使经历，完成，接通电话

> She wouldn't want to put them through the ordeal of a huge ceremony.
> 她不想让他们参加大型仪式受罪。
> I put through a long-distance call to a friend in Fuzhou this morning.
> 我今上午给在福州的一个朋友打通了一个长途电话。

② **...we found a beautiful pair of leather shoes on sale. She told me to try them on.**

在英语中"出售"使用最多的是，for sale 与 on sale 这两个词组。
on sale "出售"，与 for sale 不同，它表示的是"进入销售环节""处于被销售的状态"。

> There are 32 different kinds of chocolate on sale along with the bread and cakes.
> 有32种不同的巧克力与面包和蛋糕一起出售。
> The government will put on sale a special issue of coins today.
> 政府将于今天出售特别发行的硬币。

on sale 还可表示"廉价出售，打折出售"。

> I bought this coat on sale, for $20 less than the original price.
> 我大减价时买到这件大衣，它比原价降低20美元。

for sale 的意思是"待售""供出售"，即"用于出售"。

> These items are just for show—they're not for sale.
> 这些物品仅供展览——不卖。

经典名句 Famous Classics

1. Death is just a part of life, something we're all destined to do.

死亡是生命的一部分，是我们注定要做的一件事。

2. Sometimes, a lot of things simply cannot explain clearly; what you have to do is to follow your heart, and pray that you make the right choice.
有的时候，很多事情根本无法解释清楚，你要做的就是跟随你的内心，并祈祷自己做出的选择是正确的。

3. I don't know if we each have a destiny, or if we're all just floating around accidentally—like on a breeze.
我不懂我们是否有着各自的命运，还是只是到处随风飘荡。

4. You know some birds are not meant to be caged, their feathers are just too bright.
你知道，有些鸟儿是注定不会被关在牢笼里的，它们的每一片羽毛都闪耀着自由的光辉。

5. Hope is a good thing and maybe the best of things. And no good thing ever dies.
希望是一个好东西，也许是最好的，好东西是不会消亡的。

读书笔记

28 I Will Always Forgive You
我会永远原谅你

Brent had learned to play the piano at age four, the **clarinet** at age seven, and had just begun to play the oboe. His music teachers said he'd be a famous **musician** someday. There was only one thing at which Lisa was better than Brent — basketball. They played it almost every afternoon after school. Brent could have refused to play, but he knew that it was Lisa's only joy in the midst of her struggles to get C's and D's at school.

Brent had become all that his music teachers said he would. Few could play the **oboe** better than he. In his fourth year at the best music school in the United States, he received the opportunity of a life time — a chance to try out for New York City's great **orchestra.**

The **tryout** would be held sometime during the following two weeks. Brent had been out when the call about the tryout came to the house. Lisa was the only one home and on her way out the door, eager to get to work on time.

"Two-thirty on the tenth," the **secretary** said on the phone. Lisa did not have a pen, but she told herself that

布伦特4岁学钢琴，七岁学吹单簧管，最近开始学吹双簧管。音乐老师说他将来会成为著名的音乐家。只有一件事情丽萨比布伦特优秀，那就是打篮球。他们几乎每天下午放学都会打篮球，布伦特本可以拒绝打篮球，但是他知道这是丽萨在学校尽力得到C's和D's过程中唯一的乐趣。

布伦特成了音乐老师口中所说的样子，几乎没人比他的双簧管吹得好。在美国最好的音乐学校就读的第4年，他收到了一生中难道的一次机会——去参加纽约市最大的管弦乐队的选拔表演。

选拔表演会在接下来的2周内的某个时间进行，当电话打到家里来的时候，布伦特出去了，只有丽萨一个人在家，而且正准备出门，着急着按时上班。

"十号下午2点半"，秘书在电话里说到。丽萨当时没有笔，但是她告诉着急她能记得住。

丽萨知道她毁了布伦特的一生，他永远也不可能原谅她了，她让全家人失望了，除了离

she could remember it.

Lisa knew that she had ruined Brent's life. He could never forgive her for that. She had failed her family, and there was nothing to do but to leave home. Lisa packed her pickup truck in the middle of the night.

Lisa did not think she would ever see home again. But one day in the restaurant where she worked she saw a face she knew. "Lisa!" said Mrs. Nelson, looking up from her plate, "What a surprise!"

The woman was a friend of Lisa's family from back home. "I was so sorry to hear about your brother," Mrs. Nelson said softly, "Such a terrible accident. But we can be thankful that he died quickly. He didn't **suffer**." Lisa stared at the woman in shock.

"Wh-hat?" She finally **stammered**.

It couldn't be! Her brother? Dead? The woman quickly saw that Lisa did not know about the accident. She told the girl the sad story of the speeding car, the rush to the hospital, the doctors working over Brent. But all they could do was not enough to save him.

Lisa returned home that afternoon. Now she found herself in her room thinking about her brother as she held the small box that held some of her **memories** of him. Sadly, she opened

开家，她什么也做不了。于是，深夜丽萨把行李装车开车皮卡车走了。

丽萨心想她再也没不会回家了，但有一天在她工作的餐厅她见到了一张熟悉的面孔，"丽萨"，尼尔森太太喊道，抬起头，"太惊讶了。"

这个女人是丽萨家的朋友，"听到你弟弟的消息我非常难过"，尼尔森夫人轻声地说着，"事故太可怕了，但是很感激他走得很快，没有受罪。"丽萨非常惊讶地看着这个女人。

"什么？"她最终怔住了。

这不可能？她的弟弟？死了？这个女人很快就看出丽萨并不知道那次的事故，她告诉这个女孩那个悲惨的故事，疾驰的车，迅速送往医院，医生抢救布伦特，但是他们所做的一切也没有挽救布伦特的生命。

那天下午丽萨回家了，她发觉自己在房间里想着她的弟弟，手里拿着存有一些关于他的回忆的小盒子，悲伤地打开盒子，看了看里面。一切如初，都和她记忆中的一样，除了一样东西——布伦特原谅她的表格。

the box and peered inside. It was as she remembered, except for one item—Brent's chart.

单词解析 Word Analysis

clarinet [ˌklærəˈnet] *n.* 竖笛，单簧管

例 My brother has played the clarinet for twenty-six years.
我哥哥吹单簧管有二十六年之久。

musician [mjuˈzɪʃn] *n.* 音乐家

例 He was a brilliant musician.
他是一位才华横溢的音乐家。

oboe [ˈəʊbəʊ] *n.* 双簧管

例 The oboe and the clarinet have got certain features in common.
双簧管和单簧管有些相似之处。

orchestra [ˈɔːkɪstrə] *n.* 管弦乐队

例 Young conductors earn their spurs in a small orchestra or opera house.
年轻的指挥家们在小乐队或小歌剧院里崭露头角。

tryout [ˈtraɪaʊt] *n.* 选拔赛，试演

例 Next Monday the tryout for soccer team gonna officially starts.
下星期一足球队训练正式开始！

secretary [ˈsekrətri] *n.* 秘书

例 He liked the Secretary no better than his assistant.
他讨厌这位大臣的程度几乎和讨厌大臣的助理一样。

suffer [ˈsʌfə(r)] *v.* 遭受，经受

例 Can you assure me that my father is not suffering?
你能保证我父亲不会受罪吗？

stammer ['stæmə] v. 口吃，结巴

例 Five percent of children stammer at some point.
5%的儿童在某个时期会口吃。

memories ['memərɪz] n. 记忆力，记性（memory的复数）

例 All the details of the meeting are fresh in my memory.
我对会议的所有细节都记忆犹新。

语法知识点 Grammar Points

① **Brent could have refused to play, but he knew that it was Lisa's only joy in the midst of her struggles to get C's and D's at school.**

could have done 是一种虚拟语气，"过去本能够做某事却未做"，表示对过去事情的假设，其否定形式couldn't have done 没有虚拟语气，couldn't have done 只能表推测，相当于 can't have done，意为"过去不可能做了某事"。

例 He could have looked over the papers in less than ten minutes.
他本可在10分钟内把文件翻看一遍的。

类似结构should have done "过去本应该做某事却未做"，表达一种责备或内疚的语气，其否定结构 shouldn't have done 表示"过去本不该做某事却做了"。

例 The night shift should have been safely down the mine long ago.
上夜班的矿工本应该早就安全地到达井下了。

② **Lisa was the only one home and on her way out the door, eager to get to work on time.**

on time 按时，准时

例 He had to bring forward an 11 o'clock meeting so that he could get to the funeral on time.
他不得不把11点的会议提前，这样他就可以准时赶去参加葬礼。

in time 及时

例 I hope you get home in time, to watch your favorite show.
我希望你能及时回家，按时看你最喜欢的节目。

③ Lisa stared at the woman in shock.

in shock 震惊，吃惊地，休克

例 When I told them they were all in shock and they couldn't believe it.
当我告诉他们真相时他们都震惊到无法相信。

She is still in shock after the accident.
事故发生后到现在，她仍然处于休克状态。

经典名句 Famous Classics

1. Maybe God wants you to meet many wrong people before you meet the right one, so when this happens, you'll be thankful.
也许上帝让你在遇见那个合适的人之前遇见很多错误的人，所以，当你遇到的时候，你应心存感激。

2. It takes a strong man to save himself, and a great man to save another.
坚强的人只能救赎自己，伟大的人才能拯救他人。

3. When we move others' stumbling block, perhaps it is paving the way for ourselves.
当我们搬开别人脚下的绊脚石时，也许恰恰是在为自己铺路。

29 Stand Tall
站直了

I was filled with doubts and worries until my grandfather told me to stand tall.

I had always felt **insecure** and out of place as one of the taller members of my class, standing a head above the other girls and stooping at the back of the line to avoid sticking out.

My grandfather would watch me grow increasingly uncomfortable, but he didn't laugh at my self-consciousness or try to **console** me. Instead, he would **admonish** me.

Stand straight and tall, he'd say, as I unsuccessfully tried to **shrink** myself.

And each time, I would **sheepishly** comply. Even at age 15, I understood that his advice was about more than just feet and inches.

My grandfather grew up in war-torn Europe. After the war, he boarded a boat for America, and on January 27, 1947, he stepped onto the dock of Pier 86 in Manhattan. He was hungry and suffering from sickness. All alone in a new country, he was frightened about his future.

Still, he marched head-on into the

我满腹疑惑和担忧，直到爷爷告诉我站直了。

作为班级最高的成员之一，我总是觉得不安全和别扭，比其他女生高出一个头，总是站在队伍的后面，从而避免太过突出。

爷爷看出我因成长带来的不舒服，但是他没有嘲笑我，也没有试着安慰我，相反，他责备了我。

每次我试图缩着身子的时候，爷爷会说，挺起腰杆站直了。

每次，我总是迷迷糊糊地听他的话。甚至15岁，我就明白他的告诫不仅仅是指身高。

爷爷成长在战乱的欧洲。战争结束之后，他登上了去美国的船，1947年1月27日，他踏上了曼哈顿的86号码头。饥饿，生病，独处异国的他非常担心自己的未来。

他仍然硬着头皮前进，走进了纽约繁华的街上，不久后他遇见了其他欧洲移民，每一个人都在寻找出路。

如果他们能做到，为什

hustle and bustle of the streets of New York. Soon he met other European **immigrants**, each of them trying to find his or her own way.

If they could do it, why couldn't he! "Stand straight, stand tall," he would remind himself.

Thanks to the help of a loyal and trusting friend, my grandfather acquired a jewelry booth on Canal Street, at that time the heart of the busy diamond district in New York City. He once told me how nervous he was on that first day of work. He was not only trying to learn this tough new business, but also a new language.

To his surprise, the men in the neighboring booths — who could have taken advantage of him — offered their help and advice. Within months, my grandfather was commanding his spot behind the counter, selling diamonds and all kinds of cultured pearls as if he'd been doing it his whole life.

I am so proud to be one of those children. Listening to my grandfather's **remarkable** experiences has changed the way I view my own life.

His advice to me has become much more than a **challenge** to improve my **posture**. It tells me to be proud of who I am.

"Stand straight, stand tall," my grandfather told me.

他不能呢?"挺起腰杆,站直了",他提醒自己。

坚尼街是当时纽约最繁华的珠宝街区,多亏一位忠诚值得信任的朋友的帮忙,爷爷得到了一个珠宝摊位。爷爷曾经告诉我第一天工作的他有多么紧张。他不仅要学这个新的复杂的业务,还要学习语言。

令他惊讶的是,本可以欺负爷爷的隔壁摊位的摊主们不仅没有欺负他,还提供帮助和建议。几个月之后,爷爷就在柜台站稳了脚跟,买钻石和各种珍珠,看起来他似乎已经做这行做了一辈子。

我很自豪成为这些孩子中的一员,听爷爷的非同寻常的经历已经改变了我对自己生活的看法。

他给我的建议变成了一种改善站姿的挑战,它告诉我要引以为傲。

"挺起腰板,站直了。"外公这样告诉我。

单词解析 *Word Analysis*

insecure [ˌɪnsɪˈkjʊə(r)] *adj.* 缺乏自信的，对自己无把握的

例 Most mothers are insecure about their performance as mothers.
大多数母亲对自己为人母的表现都不是很自信。

admonish [ədˈmɒnɪʃ] *v.* 责备，警戒

例 They admonished me for taking risks with my health.
他们责备我不应拿自己的健康冒险。

console [kənˈsəʊl] *v.* 安慰，安抚

例 Often they cry, and I have to play the role of a mother, consoling them.
经常他们一哭，我就要充当母亲的角色抚慰他们。

shrink [ʃrɪŋk] *v.* 退缩，畏缩

例 One child shrinks away from me when I try to talk to him.
当我试图和一个孩子说话时，他避开了我。

sheepishly [ˈʃiːpɪʃlɪ] *adv.* 怯懦地，胆怯地

例 He just stood there, tonguetied and grinning sheepishly.
他只是张口结舌地站在那儿，羞怯地笑着。

immigrants [ˈɪmɪɡrənts] *n.* 移民

例 A wave of immigrants is washing over Western Europe.
移民潮正席卷西欧。

remarkable [rɪˈmɑːkəbl] *adj.* 引人注目的，不同寻常的

例 It was a remarkable achievement.
那是一项非凡的成就。

posture [ˈpɒstʃə(r)] *n.* 姿势，姿态

例 Exercise, fresh air, and good posture are all helpful.
锻炼、新鲜空气和好的坐立姿势都很有益。

challenge [ˈtʃæləndʒ] *n.* 挑战

例 I like big challenges and they don't come much bigger than this.
我喜欢大的挑战，而所有挑战中再没有比这更大的了。

Stand Tall 站直了 29

语法知识点 *Grammar Points*

① My grandfather would watch me grow increasingly uncomfortable, but he didn't laugh at my self-consciousness

laugh at 嘲笑，蔑视，对……满不在乎

例 You can stand there and feel superior as you point and laugh at them.
你站在那儿指指点点、嘲笑他们时，会觉得自己高人一等。

It wasn't very Christian of you to laugh at the poor child.
你嘲笑穷孩子，那可不是基督徒的所为。

② He was hungry and suffering from sickness. All alone in a new country, he was frightened about his future.

suffer from 患（某种病），受（某种病痛）折磨

例 All children will tend to suffer from separation from their parents and siblings.
所有的孩子和他们的父母及兄弟姐妹分开后往往都会难过。

Those who suffer from narcissism become self-absorbed or chronic show-offs.
被自恋症折磨的人会变得只专注于自己的事情，或者不断地自我炫耀。

be frightened about 害怕，对……感到恐惧，常用的是be frightened to。

例 He told a panicked man in Wisconsin not to be too frightened about the economic crisis.
对一个惶恐不已的威斯康星人，他说不要太过担心经济危机。

③ He was not only trying to learn this tough new business, but also a new language.

not only...but also 是英语中比较常见的一个关联词组，用于连接两个表示并列关系的成分，着重强调后者。它的意思是"不仅……而且……"；其中的also有时可以省略。可连接主语、谓语、宾语补足语、宾语、表语、状语、定语、从句等。

例 If your friend reminds you kindly of your faults, take what he says not merely pleasantly but thankfully.
如果你的朋友善意地指明你的缺点，你不但要欣然接受，而且要心怀感激之情。

155

Light and bright colors make people not only happier but more active.
浅色和鲜艳的颜色不但使人看了高兴，也会使人更加活泼。

Man has become master not only of the sky but also of the space.
人类不但征服了天空，而且征服了太空。

经典名句 Famous Classics

1. A liar is always lavish of oaths.
   骗子从不吝惜誓言。

2. We always like those who admire us; we do not always like those whom we admire.
   我们总是喜欢崇敬我们的人，但并不永远喜欢我们所崇敬的人。

3. If a man deceives me once, shame on him; if twice, shame on me.
   人欺我一次，此人可耻；欺我二次，我可耻。

4. All the splendor in the world is not worth a good friend.
   人世间所有的荣华富贵不如一个好朋友。

5. Man was born free, but everywhere he is in chains.
   人是生而自由的，却处处受到束缚。

6. Every flatterer lives at the expense of those who listen to him.
   阿谀奉承的人正是靠听信谗言的人活命的。

7. Life is to talk after a respite and not to act ahead of schedule.
   生命就是且缓一口气再讲，明天再说明天的。

8. Do not be restless; do not be hasty.
   不要魂不守舍，不要匆忙行事。

30 The Games Sisters Play
那些属于我们姐妹的游戏

My mother has yanked me from the back seat of the car out onto the **shoulder** of the highway. She clutches my wrists and glares down at me, says she's leaving me right here on the side of the road unless I promise to stop.

I stare at the cars whooshing by, at the tall sepia-colored weeds, at the little pieces of **litter** everywhere, and am terrified that she really will. I vow never to kick my baby sister in the face again.

As time went on, another sister came along, then another. Our three-bedroom split-level became full of girls—yes, four girls, all under the age of 8. It was a noisy, **chaotic** house, a place where my dad often retreated to his room for peace.

"Play with your sisters," my mother commanded on those lazy afternoons when I claimed to be bored, "I had them for you."

Though their **constant** presence had long ago eliminated the **novelty** of such a suggestion, my mother was right. My three little sisters were convenient to have around. Kickable or not, they were my constant **companions**: my

妈妈猛地把我从汽车后排座位拉到高速公路的紧急停车道上。她紧握我的手腕，愤怒地看着我说，除非我答应不再踢妹妹，否则她将会把我一个人留在高速公路上。

看着一辆辆汽车从身边飞驰，高耸的红褐色杂草以及随处可见的垃圾，我害怕她真的会那么做。我发誓再也不会踢妹妹的脸了。

接下来，妈妈又生了一个妹妹，接着又一个，我们家错层式的三居室里满是女孩——是的，4个女孩，年龄都在8岁以下。家里吵吵闹闹，杂乱一片，爸爸经常躲到房间求安静。

慵懒的下午，当我声称无聊的时候，"跟妹妹们玩去，"妈妈会命令我，"我生下她们就是为了和你玩。"

虽说她们的无时不在让我早已对妈妈的这个提议没了新鲜感，不过妈妈说得没错。我的三个妹妹都是随叫随到。不管我有没有踢她们，我都始终有她们的陪伴——她们是我

annoying, **endcaring**, **permanent** playmates.

In our one-hour-of-TV-a-day household, we relied on our imaginations for **entertainment**.

Sometimes I resented being the oldest. I hated the way I had to set a good example all the time—that, or take responsibility for everything my sisters did wrong. I hated how they followed me around and stole my clothes. I wanted to talk to my mom uninterrupted or eat a snack without having to share a bite with each sister.

But even back then I realized I was fortunate to have them, to never be lonely. We each have our own **distinct** personalities certainly, our unique talents and **ambitions**, but no one will ever understand me the way my sisters do. We have the same sense of humor, the same favorite games, and the same memories.

My sisters and I don't play gymnastics anymore—we're consumed by more serious pursuits, like job applications, ACT exams, and boyfriends. My baby sister is in high school now, and she's on Facebook. Our parents had to invest in a family plan with unlimited texting years ago, because that's how we communicate with our friends, and often, each other.

永远的玩伴，欢喜和忧愁同分享。

在每天只能看1个小时电视的家里，我们靠着想象力来娱乐。

有时候我讨厌自己是最大的，我讨厌我必须要一直给她们树立榜样，讨厌要为妹妹们做的任何错事负责，我讨厌她们总是跟着我转，偷穿我的衣服。我希望和妈妈讲话时不被打断，或者吃零食不用和每一个妹妹分享。

但是，即使在那时，我意识到了拥有她们我是幸运的，从来不会感到孤独。我们每个人都有自己独特的个性、特有的才能以及抱负，但是再不会有人像我的妹妹那样了解我。我们有着同样的幽默感，同样的最爱的游戏以及共同的记忆。

我和妹妹们再也不玩体操游戏了——因为我们有着更重要的追求，比如申请工作、参加ACT考试或者交男朋友。我最小的妹妹现在上高中了，她玩facebook。几年前，父母还不得不花钱开通无限发短信的家庭计划服务，因为发短信是我们与朋友以及彼此之间常用的交流方式。

I don't remember much else, just that I was happy.

我记不得更多的事情了，只知道那时我很快乐。

单词解析 Word Analysis

shoulder [ˈʃəʊldə(r)] *n.* 肩膀

例 She led him to an armchair, with her arm round his shoulder.
她揽着他的肩膀，将他领到一把扶手椅旁。

litter [ˈlɪtə(r)] *n.* 杂物，垃圾

例 On Wednesday we cleared a beach and woodland of litter.
星期三我们清理了一块海滨林地的垃圾。

chaotic [keɪˈɒtɪk] *adj.* 混乱的，乱糟糟的

例 My own house feels as filthy and chaotic as a bus terminal.
我自家的房子感觉又脏又乱，活像公共汽车终点站。

constant [ˈkɒnstənt] *adj.* 持续不断的，重复的，一直存在的

例 She suggests that women are under constant pressure to be abnormally thin.
她暗示说女性总是处在保持身材异常瘦削的压力之下。

novelty [ˈnɒvlti] *n.* 新奇性，新颖，新奇的事物

例 It came from the days when a motor car was a novelty.
这要从轿车还是新鲜玩意儿那会儿说起。

companion [kəmˈpænjən] *n.* 同伴，伴侣

例 Fred had been her constant companion for the last six years of her life.
在她生命的最后6年，弗莱德一直是她忠实的伴侣。

annoying [əˈnɔɪɪŋ] *adj.* 令人厌烦的，令人生气的

例 The annoying thing about the scheme is that it's confusing.
这项计划可气的地方是它让人一头雾水。

endearing [ɪnˈdɪərɪŋ] *adj.* 惹人喜爱的，可爱的
- She has such an endearing personality.
  她的个性非常讨人喜欢。

permanent [ˈpɜːmənənt] *adj.* 永久的，永恒的
- Heavy drinking can cause permanent damage to the brain.
  酗酒能造成永久性大脑损伤。

distinct [dɪˈstɪŋkt] *adj.* 有区别的，不同的
- This book is divided into two distinct parts.
  这本书分为内容不同的两部分。

ambition [æmˈbɪʃən] *n.* 梦想，理想；抱负，野心
- His ambition is to sail round the world.
  他的梦想是环球航行。

语法知识点 Grammar Points

① She clutches my wrists and glares down at me, says she's leaving me right here on the side of the road unless I promise to stop.

right 在句中为副词，表示恰当地，正好地
- The accident happened right over there.
  事故正好发生在那里。
  When it comes to piano-playing he's right there.
  要是说到弹钢琴，那他可在行呢。

right 除可做副词外，还可做形容词、名词以及动词。
- You were quite right to criticize him.
  你批评他批评得很对。（作形容词）
  I have the right to ask for an explanation.
  我有权要求一个解释。（作名词）
  Give me one more chance to right my mistakes, please.
  请再给我一次机会纠正错误吧。（作动词）

② I hated the way I had to set a good example all the time—that, or take responsibility for everything my sisters did wrong.

set a good example 做模范，树立榜样

例 Teachers should restrain themselves so as to set a good example.
教师应当躬行自律，以垂范学生。

Worry and dread are a waste of time and do not set a good example for others.
忧虑与恐惧都是在浪费时间，也没有为其他人做个好榜样。

经典名句 Famous Classics

1. One's courtesy is a mirror to see his image.
   一个人的礼貌是一面照出他肖像的镜子。

2. Those who cannot do trivial things can not accomplish great things.
   不会做小事的人，也做不出大事来。

3. Better to remain silent and be thought a fool than to speak out and remove all doubt.
   做一个消除一切疑虑的出头鸟，还不如保持沉默被当成傻子。

4. Everything you see exists together in a delicate balance.
   世界上所有的生命都在微妙的平衡中生存。

5. A house divided against itself cannot stand.
   一个分裂的家是没有立足之地的。

6. And in the end, it's not the years in your life that count. It's the life in your years.
   最后，重要的不是你活了多久，而是怎么活。

7. Nearly all men can stand adversity, but if you want to test a man's character, give him power.
   几乎所有的人都能忍受逆境，但如果你想测试一个人的性格，那就给他权力。

8. Character is like a tree and reputation a shadow. The shadow is what we think of it; the tree is the real thing.
   人品就像是树，而声誉是树荫。我们想到的是树荫，而树才是本体。

31 The Meanest Mother
无情的母亲

I had the meanest mother in the whole world. While other kids ate candy for breakfast, I had to have cereal, eggs or toast. When others had cokes and candy for lunch, I had to eat a sandwich. As you can guess, my supper was different from the other kids' also. But at least, I wasn't alone in my **sufferings**. My sister and two brothers had the same **mean** mother as I did.

My mother insisted upon knowing where we were at all times. You'd think we were on a chain gang. She had to know who our friends were and where we were going. She insisted if we said we'd be gone an hour, that we be gone one hour or less—not one hour and one minute.

We had to wear clean clothes and take a bath. The other kids always wore their clothes for days. We reached the height of **insults** because she made our clothes herself, just to save money.

The worst is yet to come. We had to be in bed by nine each night and up at eight the next morning. We couldn't sleep till noon like our friends. So while they slept—my mother actually had the

我有全世界最无情的妈妈。其他孩子早餐吃糖果，我必须吃燕麦、鸡蛋或者吐司；其他孩子午饭喝可乐、吃糖果，我必须吃三明治。如你所料，我的晚饭和别的孩子也不同。但是，至少我不是孤军奋战，我的姐姐和两个兄弟和我一样有一个无情的妈妈。

我的妈妈坚持实时掌握我们的行踪。你会认为我们是一帮被拴在一根链子上的囚犯。她必须知道我们的朋友是谁以及我们打算去哪里。她坚持认为，如果我们说出去1个小时，那就必须是1个小时或者少于1个小时，不能是1个小时零1分钟。

我们必须穿干净的衣服，必须洗澡。其他的孩子总是一件衣服穿好多天。最让我们感到丢人的是，只是为了省钱，她自己给我们做衣服。

最糟糕的事情是，我们每天晚上9点前必须睡觉，早上8点前必须起床。我们不能像朋友们一样睡到中午。因此，他们睡觉时，我的妈妈实际正在

The MEANEST Mother
无情的母亲

nerve to break the Child Labor Law. She made us work. We had to wash dishes, make beds, learn to cook, all sorts of **cruel** things. I believe she laid awake at night thinking up mean things to do to us.

Through the years, things didn't improve a bit. We could not lie in bed, "sick" like our friends did, and miss school. Our marks in school had to be up to par. Our friends' report cards had beautiful colors on them, black for passing, red for failing. My mother, being as different as she was, would settle for nothing less than **ugly** black marks.

As the years rolled by, first one and then the other of us was put to **shame**. We were graduated from high school. With our mother behind us, talking, hitting and demanding respect, none of us was allowed the pleasure of being a **drop-out**.

My mother was a complete failure as a mother. Out of four children, a couple of us attained some higher education. None of us have ever been arrested or divorced. Each of my brothers served his time in the service of this country.

She forced us to grow up into God-fearing, educated, honest adults. Using this as a **background**, I am now trying

触犯童工法，她让我们劳动。我们必须洗碗，整理床铺，学习做饭等各种残酷的事情。我相信她熬夜不睡是想着如何无情地折磨我们。

多年来，事情没有一点点的改观。我们不能像朋友们一样躺在床上装病逃课，我们的在学校的成绩必须达标，朋友们的成绩单上有各种漂亮的颜色，黑色代表及格，红色代表不及格。而我的妈妈在这一点上仍是与众不同，她只满足于那些难看的黑乎乎的分数。

一年年过去了，我们一个接着一个被置于无地自容。高中毕业了，妈妈在我们身后，说教、打骂并要求尊重，我们中没人享受过辍学的乐趣。

作为一个母亲，我妈妈是个彻头彻尾的失败者。4个孩子中有2个孩子接受了高等教育，没人被捕，没人离婚。我的哥哥们都服了兵役，为国效力。

她迫使我们成长为虔诚的、有教养的、诚实的成年人。利用这种成长背景，我试着养育我的三个孩子。现在，当孩子说我无情的时候，我会充满骄傲。为什么呢？因为现在的每一天我都感谢上帝赐予了我全世界最无情的妈妈。

to raise my three children. I am filled with pride when my children call me mean. Why? Because now I thank God every day for giving me the meanest mother in the whole world.

单词解析 Word Analysis

sufferings ['sʌfərɪŋz] *n.* （肉体或内心的）痛苦，苦难，折磨

例 They began to recover slowly from their nightmare of pain and suffering.
他们开始从痛苦的梦魇中慢慢恢复过来。

mean [miːn] *adj.* 吝啬的，小气的，刻薄的

例 The girls had locked themselves in upstairs because Mack had been mean to them.
姑娘们把自己锁在楼上，因为麦克对她们很刻薄。

insult [in'sʌlt] *n.* 侮辱，辱骂

例 Their behavior was an insult to the people they represent.
他们的行为是对他们代表的人民的一种侮辱。

cruel [kruːəl] *adj.* 残酷的，冷酷的，残忍的

例 Don't you think it's cruel to cage a creature up?
你不认为把动物关进笼里太残忍了吗？

ugly ['ʌgli] *adj.* 丑陋的，难看的

例 She makes me feel dowdy and ugly.
她让我自惭形秽。

shame [ʃeɪm] *n.* 羞愧，羞辱

例 They feel shame and guilt as though it is their fault.
他们觉得羞愧和内疚，就好像这是他们的错。

The Meanest Mother 无情的母亲 31

drop-out *n.* 辍学

> You'll never go to college if you have a drop-out in high school.
> 如果高中辍学，你就永远不能上大学了。

background ['bækgraʊnd] *n.* 背景，学历，经历

> She came from a working-class background.
> 她出身于工人家庭。

语法知识点 Grammar Points

① **My mother insisted upon knowing where we were at all times.**

insist on doing sth. 坚持要求做某事。

> If you insist on doing so, then we have to work overtime.
> 如果你坚持要这么做，那么我们只好加班了。

insist on/upon 后面可直接跟名词，表示"坚决要求"。

> We insisted on a refund of the full amount.
> 我们坚持要求全额退款。

② **I believe she laid awake at night thinking up mean things to do to us.**

awake 醒着的，形容词做表语。

> I was still awake when he came to bed.
> 他就寝时我还没有入睡。

这个单词也有动词的用法，awake to sth. 察觉到，意识到。

> It took her some time to awake to the dangers of her situation.
> 过了一些时间她才意识到处境危险。

③ **Out of four children, a couple of us attained some higher education. None of us have ever been arrested or divorced.**

out of 由于；用……（材料）；自……离开；得自（来源）。

> You scared us out of our wits. We heard you had an accident.
> 你把我们吓坏了，我们听说你出事了。
>
> I decided to paint the bathroom ceiling but ran out of steam halfway through.
> 我决定粉刷一下浴室的天花板，但干了一半就精疲力竭了。

Out of deference to him, I lowered my head as he prayed.
出于对他的敬重,在他祈祷时我低下了头。

a couple of 两个,几个

例 I almost lasted the two weeks. I only had a couple of days to do.
我几乎撑过了这两个星期。我只有几天时间去做。

He had lent the bungalow to the Conrads for a couple of weeks.
他把那间平房借给康拉德一家住了两三个星期。

经典名句 Famous Classics

1. Love is when the other person's happiness is more important than your own.
   爱情就是把别人的幸福看得比自己的重要。

2. Gravitation is not responsible for people falling in love.
   并非地球引力使人坠入爱河。

3. There are still many causes worth sacrificing for, so much history yet to be made.
   还有许多东西是值得牺牲的,还有这么多的历史等着我们去创造。

4. The unexamined life is not worth living.
   没有反省的人生不值得活。

5. When the world turns its back on you, you turn your back on the world.
   如果这个世界对你不理不睬,你也可以这样对待它。

读书笔记

32 Just What My Father Always Wanted
总能让爸爸高兴的礼物

No matter how **humble** the contents of a package, Dad always took care to appreciate the time and thought that went into selecting a store-bought gift or the skill that went into making one. When we were young and had no money to buy Dad gifts, we often relied on imagination to make up for a shortage of shopping funds. Dad beamed with pleasure upon opening a coin pouch made at summer camp, a note **redeemable** for washing and waxing his car, or a homemade card with a message of a prayer said in his honor.

But even when our buying power increased through money from odd jobs and baby-sitting, we sometimes ran short on imagination. Still, Dad made our bland gifts seem like dreams come true. When he opened a plain white shirt just like the ones he wore to work, he would appear **delightfully** jolted as if he'd never seen anything like it. He'd pull the shirt out of the bag reverently and comment on its features. "Oh, this is really nice," he'd say, pointing out the button-down collar or extra-long

无论包裹里的东西有多么的不起眼，爸爸总是注意赞赏我们在挑选礼物时所花的时间和心思，或者表扬我们在制作礼物时所用的技能。小时候没钱给爸爸买礼物，我们通常依靠想象力来弥补缺乏购物资金。打开夏令营时制作的零钱包，收到一张纸条，纸条上许诺为他洗车以及给车打蜡，或者自制的祝他好运的贺卡，爸爸总是很开心。

靠着打零工和替人看孩子的收入增加了我们的购买力，但是有些时候想象力缺乏。即便如此，爸爸仍让我们觉得收到乏味礼物似乎梦想成真了。当他收到一件普通的白色衬衫，无异于他平常上班穿的，他会表现的非常高兴，似乎他从来没有见过这种东西。他会小心翼翼地从盒子里拿出衬衫，并对衬衫的特点评论一番。"哇，太漂亮了"，他会指着缝有纽扣的领尖或者特别加长的燕尾说道。接着，他会小心的去掉包装试穿一下。"这正是我想要整的"，这句话他会赞扬其精细的做工以及整洁的布料的同时重复好几次。个过程中，

shirttail. Then he'd carefully remove the packaging and try it on. "It's exactly what I needed," he'd say several times in between praising the quality of workmanship and **tidiness** of the fabric. All the while, we watched, wallowing in the pleasure of pleasing Dad.

Over the years, we gave Dad a full closet of shirts—plaid flannels for the cold, short-sleeved knits for golf, and long-sleeved Oxford shirts for church and work. We gave him miles of ties. We gave him implements of leisure such as golf balls and gloves and fishing poles, and things to nurture hobbies like tools for woodworking and gardening.

If the color or size wasn't perfect, or if his toolbox already held in **triplicate** the tool we gave him, Dad didn't let on. He made us feel so good about our gifts that Father's Day became an occasion we all looked forward to.

I suspect Dad was always more comfortable with giving gifts than receiving them. I figure that's what made him so good at appreciating our simple gifts—his ever-present **awareness** that every gift that comes to you brings an opportunity to give one back in the form of **gratitude**.

Dad's manner of receiving even the most **mediocre** of presents was a

我们一直注视着，沉醉在取悦爸爸的快乐之中。

这些年来，我们送给爸爸的衬衫装满了整个衣柜——天冷穿的格子图案的法兰绒衬衣，打高尔夫球时穿的短袖衬衣，去教堂和上班时穿的长袖牛津布衬衣。我们送了她无数条领带，我们送了她各种娱乐工具，高尔夫球，手套，钓鱼竿以及培养爱好的东西，比如园艺和木工的工具。

如果颜色或尺寸不合适，或者我们送了一件他工具箱里已有三件的工具，爸爸也不会表露出来。对于我们送的礼物，他总是让我们感觉非常的好，以至于我们都很期待父亲节的到来。

比起收礼物，赠送礼物更让爸爸感到舒服，我猜。我想那正是他欣赏我们简单的礼物的原因——他一直都知道每次收到礼物我们都有机会用"表示感激"这种方式回馈对方。

即使是收到最普通的礼物的态度，对爸爸来说，也是我们家里一份朴素而持久的礼物。虽然他已经不在了，但他的礼物依然活在我们的记忆中。

simple but enduring gift for our family. Although he is no longer with us, his gift lives on in our memories.

单词解析 *Word Analysis*

humble ['hʌmbl] *adj.* 谦逊的，谦虚的，谦卑的

- He gave a great performance, but he was very humble.
  他的表演非常出色，但他却很谦虚。

redeemable [rɪ'diːməbl] *adj.* 可兑换的，可交换的

- Their full catalogue costs $5, redeemable against a first order.
  他们的完整目录售价5美元，第一次订购时可返还这5美元。

delightfully [dɪ'laɪtfəlɪ] *adv.* 令人高兴地，使人愉快地

- The old view of Galileo was delightfully uncomplicated.
  过去对伽利略的看法并不复杂（指不深奥），这是令人欣然的。

shirttail ['ʃɜːtteɪl] *n.* 衬衫的下摆

- He wore sandals and old jeans and his shirt-tails weren't tucked in.
  他穿着凉鞋、旧仔裤，衬衫下摆也没塞进裤子里。

tidiness ['taɪdɪnəs] *n.* 整齐，整洁

- He preferred the cleanness and tidiness of the wild sod.
  他喜欢荒野草地的清洁和整齐。

triplicate ['trɪplɪkət] *n.* 一式三份

- Fill out this from in triplicate.
  把这表格一式三份填好。

awareness [ə'weənəs] *n.* 觉悟，意识

- Deep inside the awareness was stirring that something was about to happen.
  内心深处隐隐感觉到有什么事即将发生。

gratitude [ˈgrætɪtjuːd] *n.* 感谢，感恩之情

例 I wish to express my gratitude to Kathy Davis for her immense practical help.
凯茜·戴维斯实实在在地帮了大忙，我想对她表示感谢。

mediocre [ˌmiːdiˈəʊkə(r)] *adj.* 普通的，平庸的，一般的

例 His school record was mediocre.
他在学校成绩平平。

语法知识点 *Grammar Points*

① **When we were young and had no money to buy Dad gifts, we often relied on imagination to make up for a shortage of shopping funds.**

rely on 依靠，依赖；信赖，信任

例 We had to rely on a compass and a lot of luck to get here.
我们不得不依靠指南针和不错的运气找到这儿来。

You can't rely on any figures you get from them.
你不能相信从他们那儿得到的任何数据。

make up for 弥补，补偿

例 Ask for an extra compensation payment to make up for the stress you have been caused.
为补偿你为此承受的压力，你要申请额外的补偿金。

Her beauty can't make up for her stupidity.
她的美丽不能弥补她的愚蠢。

② **We gave him miles of ties. We gave him implements of leisure such as...**

miles of 数英里

例 I would include my city since I only work within 50 miles of home.
由于工作范围只在附近50英里以内，所以关键词中包含我的城市。

Just What My Father Always Wanted
总能让爸爸高兴的礼物 32

> ③ Although he is no longer with us, his gift lives on in our memories.

no longer 不再，已不

例 After about three months, I was no longer addicted to nicotine.
大约3个月后，我就不再对尼古丁上瘾了。

no more 和 not any more 可以彼此互换，意思是"不再……"，no longer 和 not any longer 也可以彼此替换，意思也是"不再……"，但 no more 偏重于指程度，no longer 偏重于指时间。

例 I am so tired that I can walk no more.
我太累了，一点也走不动了。

经典名句 Famous Classics

1. Love is a touch and yet not a touch.
   爱是想触碰却又收回的手。

2. True life is lived when tiny changes occur.
   真正的生活源于细微的改变。

3. Genius is the recovery of childhood at will.
   天才就是随心所欲地重获童心的能力。

4. The price of greatness is responsibility.
   伟大的代价就是责任。

5. Whether you come from a council estate or a country estate, your success will be determined by your own confidence and fortitude.
   无论你来自城市还是乡村，你的成功将取决于你自己的信心和坚定。

6. Living without an aim is like sailing without a compass.
   生活而无目标，犹如航海之无指南针。

7. We soon believe what we desire.
   我们欲望中的东西，我们很快就信以为真。

8. A bird in the hand is worth two in the bush.
   手中的一只鸟胜于林中的两只鸟。

33 The Memorable Cooler
冷藏箱里的难忘回忆

Grandmother's house was the favorite holiday **destination** for Tisha's family. They would load up the car and make the long drive to a farm located deep in rural south Georgia. The trip was always fun. Tisha and her two sisters played road games on the way. These consisted of playing "I spy", making faces at passing motorists, spotting interesting billboards, singing loudly along with the radio and counting various colors of cars on the road. They always had fun and the trip seemed to fly by.

Tisha and her sisters always fell asleep before reaching grandmother's house. They would awaken to car doors opening and grandmother calling out "Here you are!" They would **explode** into the farm house that looked small from the outside, but was actually perfect, large and very comfortable. Grandfather and Tisha's father would often go on hunting and fishing trips together. On one occasion, they came back from one such trip and they left a huge red cooler open in grandmother's kitchen. It was empty except for a small

祖母家是帝莎一家最喜欢的度假胜地。他们会把行李装上车，长途驱车来到位于佐治亚州南部农村深处的一个农场。旅途总是充满欢乐，帝莎和她的两个姐妹一路上玩旅途游戏，这些游戏包括"眼力大比拼"、朝路过的汽车司机做鬼脸、寻找有趣的广告牌、跟着收音机大声唱歌以及数路上的车都有哪些颜色。她们总是会玩得很开心，旅途似乎也过得很快。

帝莎和姐姐们总是在到达祖母家之前就会睡着，伴着打开车门的声音以及祖母的"你们来啦"，她们就会醒来。然后，她们会一下子冲进农场的房子，农场的房子从外面看起来很小，但实际上很大、很完美、很舒适。祖父和帝莎的爸爸经常会一起去狩猎和钓鱼。有一次，他们狩猎钓鱼回来忘记把奶奶厨房一个很大的红色冷藏箱门关上了，冷藏箱是空的，只在侧边挂了一条小毛巾。

The Memorable Cooler
冷藏箱里的难忘回忆

towel hanging off the side.

Tisha spotted the empty cooler in the kitchen and she loved to play hide and seek. She climbed into the cooler, closed the lid and could still see out of it because the towel kept it from closing all of the way. She remembered thinking how much fun it would be for the family to not know where she was. She watched the activity in the kitchen for a while and then fell asleep. She woke up an hour or so later.

Tisha heard her father ask anyone had seen her. Then she heard her grandfather come in, and saw his **tan** colored pants and boots that he always wore. They came closer to the cooler. She held her breath waiting. She could not wait anymore. About the same time that her grandfather reached down to open the cooler, she sat up, flinging the lid open and saying "Boo!" The look on his face was **priceless**. He started laughing and Tisha was delighted. Her father was also in the kitchen and he started laughing, too. She had gotten them good. The entire family **converged** in the kitchen to see what was up. Mom was not amused. Neither was grandmother.

Tisha's sisters were in **awe** that she pulled off such a wonderful **prank** and

帝莎发现了厨房的这个空的冷藏箱，喜欢玩捉迷藏的帝莎爬进了冷藏箱，关上门，仍然能看见外面的动静，因为毛巾让冷藏箱无法关严。她想着家人不知道她去哪儿了会是件多么有趣的事儿。她观察了一会儿厨房里的活动就睡着了，大约1个小时后她醒了。

帝莎听见爸爸在问有没有人见过她，接着，她听到祖父走了进来，看到祖父常穿的棕黄色裤子和靴子。他们离冷藏箱越来越近了，帝莎屏住呼吸等着，她再也等不及了，祖父伸手开冷藏箱门的同时帝莎坐了起来，猛地打开冷藏箱的门，还发出"嘘"的声音。祖父脸上的表情特别有趣，他大笑起来，帝莎也高兴起来，爸爸也在厨房大笑起来。帝莎把他们都捉弄了。全家人一起涌至厨房看发生了什么事情，妈妈没有笑，祖母也没有笑。

帝莎制造了这样一出精彩的恶作剧，还让祖父和爸爸大吃一惊，帝莎的姐姐们看到这种情况都惊呆了。那时候帝莎只有4岁，那件事情之后奶奶家的著名的红色冷藏箱就被禁用了。后来，帝莎和冷藏箱的故事成为帝莎能够回想起的最初的记忆之一，这是一段快乐的

surprised their grandfather and father. Tisha was only four years old at the time. The famous red cooler was banned from grandmother's house after that memorable event. Later, Tisha and the red **cooler** incident would be one of the first memories she could remember. It was a good one. She cherishes her first memory of love and laughter with her grandfather. First **childhood** memories really stick with you. Tisha knows this for a fact. She still can't pass by a red cooler without smiling, to this very day. It was a very **memorable** cooler.

记忆，帝莎很珍惜这份充满祖父的爱和笑声的记忆。最初的童年记忆真的可以伴随人的一生。对于这一点，帝莎坚信不疑，直到今天，她每次经过那个红色冷藏库还会禁不住笑起来，那是一个让人非常难忘的冷藏箱。

单词解析 Word Analysis

destination [ˌdestɪˈneɪʃn] *n.* 目的地，终点

例 Spain is still our most popular holiday destination.
西班牙仍是我们最喜爱的度假去处。

explode [ɪkˈspləʊd] *v.* （使）爆炸

例 They were clearing up when the second bomb exploded.
他们正在清理时，第二颗炸弹爆炸了。

tan [tæn] *adj.* 黄褐色的，棕黄色的

例 These shoes are tan, not dark brown.
这些鞋是棕黄色的，不是深褐色的。

priceless [ˈpraɪsləs] *adj.* 无价的，极为贵重的

例 They are priceless, unique and irreplaceable.
它们是独一无二、不可替代的无价之宝。

converge [kənˈvɜːdʒ] *v.* 汇集，集中，聚集

例 Hundreds of coaches will converge on the capital.

The Memorable Cooler
冷藏箱里的难忘回忆

数百辆长途汽车将会在首都汇集。

awe [ɔː] *n.* 敬畏；畏怯
- His fellow officers regarded him with awe as some sort of genius.
  同事们很敬畏他，视他如天才。

prank [præŋk] *n.* 恶作剧
- The dean was ranking the boys for pulling the prank.
  系主任正在惩罚那些恶作剧的男学生。

cooler ['kuːlə(r)] *n.* 冷藏箱，冷却
- There is a cooler in the kitchen.
  厨房里有个冷藏箱。

childhood ['tʃaɪldhʊd] *n.* 童年，幼年时代
- He was remembering a story heard in childhood.
  他在回忆儿时听过的一个故事。

memorable ['memərəbl] *adj.* 值得纪念的，难忘的
- November 30 was for me a crowded and memorable day.
  11月30日对我来说，是一个非常忙碌而且值得纪念的日子。

语法知识点 Grammar Points

① **These consisted of playing "I spy", making faces at passing motorists, spotting interesting billboards, singing loudly along with the radio and counting various colors of cars on the road.**

consist of 包括；由……组成
- The division will consist of two tank companies and one infantry company.
  这个师的组成部队将包括两个坦克连和一个步兵连。
- The British Parliament consists of the House of Commons and the House of Lords.
  英国国会是由下议院和上议院组成的。

英语中几个类似的短语，compose of，make up of，consist of。
consist of "由……构成"，与其他两个短语的区别在于，consist of 不可用于被动语态，其他两个可以，即consist of 没有be consisted of结构，其他两个词都有：be composed of, be made up of。

例 Business processes can be composed of services and other business processes.
业务流程可由服务和其他业务流程来组成。
A car is made up of different parts.
一辆车是由不同的零件组成的。

make faces at 对……做鬼脸
例 It is easy to make faces at the sun.
对太阳做鬼脸是最容易不过的。
I made sure that I was there to make faces at her as she spoke her vows.
我确信，我在那儿冲她做鬼脸，是因为她说所立下的誓言。

② **Tisha heard her father ask had anyone seen her. Then she heard her grandfather come in…**

hear sb. do sth. 听见某人做了某事，强调听见整个过程，属于一种回忆性描述。
例 I heard him go downstairs.
我听见他下了楼。

hear sb. doing sth. 听见这个动作正在进行
例 When I passed her room, I heard her singing an English song.
我路过她房间的时候，听见她在唱英文歌。

③ **Mom was not amused. Neither was grandmother.**

neither 两者都不
例 I have never been abroad, neither [nor] have I ever wished to go.
我从未去过国外，我也从未想去。

经典名句 Famous Classics

1. A man may lead a horse to the water, but he cannot make it drink.

一个人可以把马带到河边，但他不能令它饮水。

2. One cannot eat one's cake and have it.
   一个人不能把他的糕饼吃掉之后还留在手上。

3. Anything one man can imagine, other men can make it real.
   但凡人能想象到的事物，必定有人能将它实现。

4. Early to bed and early to rise, makes a man healthy, wealthy, and wise.
   早睡早起使人健康、富裕又聪明。

5. Life is just a series of trying to make up your mind.
   生活只是由一系列下决心的努力所构成。

6. All human wisdom is summed up in two words—wait and hope.
   人类所有的智慧可以归结为两个词——等待和希望。

7. It is not enough to be industrious, so are the ants. What are you industrious for?
   光勤劳是不够的，蚂蚁也是勤劳的。要看你为什么而勤劳。

8. You have to believe in yourself. That's the secret of success.
   人必须相信自己，这是成功的秘诀。

读书笔记

34 Your Name in Gold
金制你的名字

Anne's older sister, Mary, sat across from her, reading the other side of the cereal box. "Hey, Anne," she said, "Look at this **awesome** prize—'your name in gold'."

As Mary read on, Anne's interest in the prize grew. "Just send in one dollar with proof-of-purchase seal from this box and spell out your first name on the information **blank**. We will send you a special pin with your name spelled in gold. (Only one per family, please.)"

Ann grabbed the box and looked on the back, her eyes brightening with **excitement**. "That's a neat idea," she said. "A pin with my very own name spelled out in gold. I'm going to send in for it."

"Sorry, Anne, I saw it first", said Mary, "so I get first **dibs** on it. Besides, you don't have a dollar to send in, and I do."

"You always get your way—just because you're older than me", said Anne, her lower lip **trembling** as her eyes filled with tears. "Just go ahead and send in for it. See if I care!" She threw down her spoon and ran from the

安妮的姐姐玛丽坐在安妮对面，读着燕麦盒子另一面上的印字。"嗨，安妮"，她说，"看这个令人惊叹的奖品——'金制你的名字'"。

随着玛丽往下读，安妮对奖品的兴趣越发增加。"只需将一美元随盒子上的购买证明签章一起寄来，在信息栏空白处拼出您的名字，我们就会寄您一个特殊的金制着你名字的别针（每家仅限一份）"。

安妮抓住盒子，看着盒子背面，激动的眼睛闪闪发光。"很棒的主意"，她说，"一枚别针，上面金制着我的名字，我要申请这个奖品"。

"对不起，安妮，是我先看到的"，玛丽说，"因此，我有优先权，除此以外，你没有1美元，我有。"

"你总是这么霸道，就只因为你比我大"，安妮说着，下唇在颤抖，眼里充满泪水，"你去申领啊，看我会不会在乎。"说完，安妮扔掉了勺子，跑出了厨房。

几个星期之后的一天，邮递员拿来了一个小包裹，收件人是

Your Name in Gold
金制你的名字

kitchen.

Several weeks passed. One day the **mailman** brought a small package addressed to Mary. Anne was dying to see the pin, but she wouldn't let Mary know how eager she was. Mary took the package to her room. Anne **casually** followed her in and sat on the bed.

"Well, I guess they sent you your pin. I sure hope you like it." Anne said in a **mean** voice. Mary slowly took the paper off the package. She opened a little white box and carefully lifted off the top layer of white cotton.

"Oh, it's beautiful!" Mary said. "Just like the cereal box said, 'Your name in gold.' Four beautiful letters. Would you like to see it, Anne?"

"No, I don't care about your **dumb** old pin."

Mary put the white box on the **dresser** and went downstairs.

Anne was alone in the bedroom. Soon she couldn't wait any longer, so she walked over to the dresser. As she looked in the small white box, she gasped. Mixed feelings of love for her sister and shame at herself welled up within her, and the pin became a sparkling gold blur through her tears.

There on the pin were four beautiful letters—her name in gold: A-N-N-E.

玛丽。安妮非常想看下那枚别针，但是她不想让玛丽知道她的渴望。玛丽把包裹拿进了房间，安妮像平常一样跟着玛丽进了房间坐在了床上。

"嗯，我猜他们给你寄了别针，我当然希望你喜欢啦。"安妮冷言冷语地说。玛丽慢慢地去掉包裹的包装纸，打开一个白色的小盒子，小心翼翼地掀开上面铺的那层白棉布。

"好漂亮呀！"玛丽说，"跟燕麦盒子上说的一样，'金制你的名字'，四个漂亮的字母，你看到了吗，安妮？"

"不，我没在意你的又蠢又旧的别针"。

玛丽把白盒子放在梳妆台上，然后下楼去了。

安妮一个人待在卧室，不久她就按捺不住了，所以，她走到梳妆台前。看着那个小的白色盒子，她一下子愣住了，心中五味陈杂，对姐姐的爱，同时为自己的行为感到羞愧，那枚别针也在她的泪眼里模糊成了闪闪发光的一团金黄色。

别针上印着四个漂亮的字母，是金制的她的名字——A-N-N-E。

单词解析 *Word Analysis*

awesome [ˈɔːsəm] *adj.* 令人敬畏的，心生畏惧的
- The church in Ireland has always exercised an awesome power.
  爱尔兰的教堂一直掌握着令人敬畏的权力。

blank [blæŋk] *n.* 空白处，空格
- Put a word in each blank to complete the sentence.
  每个空格填上一个单词，把句子补充完整。

excitement [ɪkˈsaɪtmənt] *n.* 兴奋，激动
- The happiness and the excitement had been drained completely from her voice.
  幸福和激动已经完全从她的声音中消失了。

dibs [dɪbz] *n.* 权利；零钱
- I've got dibs on the backseat when we drive home.
  我们开车回家时，我有坐后座的权利。

tremble [ˈtrembl] *v.* 颤抖，战栗，哆嗦
- His mouth became dry, his eyes widened, and he began to tremble all over.
  他嘴唇发干，眼睛圆睁，全身开始颤抖起来。

mailman [ˈmeɪlmæn] *n.* 邮递员
- The mailman just dropped some mails in our box.
  邮差刚刚塞进一些信件在我们的信箱。

casually [ˈkæʒʊəlɪ] *adv.* 偶然地，漫不经心地
- It's difficult for me to casually deal with anything.
  要我轻松处事很难。

mean [miːn] *adj.* 不友好的，刻薄的
- The girls had locked themselves in upstairs because Mack was mean to them.
  小姑娘们把自己锁在楼上，因为麦克对她们很刻薄。

dumb [dʌm] *adj.* 愚蠢的，令人心烦的

例 I came up with this dumb idea.
我想出了这个馊主意。

dresser ['dresə(r)] *n.* 梳妆台

例 Elaine braced herself against the dresser and looked in the mirror.
伊莱恩紧贴着衣橱照镜子。

语法知识点 *Grammar Points*

① **"You always get your way—just because you're older than me," said Anne...**

get your way 随心所欲，按你的意愿发展

例 You are not always going to get your way, so don't expect to. Don't plan on everything to come out perfect.
事情总不会都如人所愿,所以不要做这样的期望。不要期待着一切都完美。

You always get your way.
你一直都是为所欲为。

② **Anne was dying to see the pin, but she wouldn't let Mary know how eager she was.**

be dying to do 渴望，极想做某事

例 You don't know how terribly I was dying to meet you again.
我是多么多么想再见到你啊。

By now I know you're dying to know what it is and where you can get one.
说到这，我知道你们非常想知道礼物是什么，从哪里可以买到。

③ **Mixed feelings of love for her sister and shame at herself welled up within her, and the pin became a sparkling gold blur through her tears.**

shame at 对……感到羞愧

例 She was covered with shame at her failure.
她对自己的失败感到无比惭愧。

She was full of shame at her bad behavior and hung her head in shame.

她为自己的不良行为感到羞愧，惭愧地低下了头。

经典名句 Famous Classics

1. Actions speak louder than words.
   事实胜于雄辩。

2. The biggest communication problem is we do not listen to understand. We listen to reply.
   最大的沟通问题是，我们聆听不是为了了解，我们聆听只为了回答。

3. Time goes by so fast; people go in and out of your life. Don't miss the opportunity to tell them the meaning in your life.
   时间在流逝，生命中人来人往。不要错失机会，告诉他们在你生命中的意义。

4. Tears: a liquid. Sometimes, only with the liquid washed, and our eyes can see clearly.
   眼泪：一种液体。有时候，唯有用该液体清洗过，我们的眼睛才能看得清楚。

5. Whatever comes, I'll love you, just as I do now. Until I die.
   无论发生什么事，我都会像现在一样爱你，直到永远。

6. The worst way to miss someone is to be seated by his/her side and know you'll never have him/her.
   错过一个人最可怕的方式就是坐在他/她的身旁，你却知道永远都不会拥有他/她。

读书笔记

35 Papa's New Pants
爸爸的新裤子

Papa saw purple pants at the market. He told the **shopkeeper**, "We're having a picnic tomorrow. I must have those pants."

When Papa tried them on, the shopkeeper said, "A perfect fit. A little long, but don't worry. They need to be shortened only the length of a thumb."

Papa paid for them and went home. He asked his wife, "Can you **hem** my new pants before the picnic tomorrow? They need to be shortened only the length of a thumb. I'd do it myself, but I make such a mess when I sew ."

Mama said, "Can't you see how busy I am? If we're going to have a picnic, first I must bake the cakes. Then I must cut tomatoes and cucumbers for the salad."

"I can see how busy you are," Papa sighed. "I'll ask Nina."

He found his oldest daughter going out the door with her **satche**l. "Nina, can you **shorten** my pants for tomorrow? They need to be cut only the length of a thumb."

Oh, Papa, Nina said, "look at this list Mama gave me. First I must go

爸爸在街上看到了一条紫色的裤子，他告诉店员，"明天我们要去野餐，我必须穿这条裤子"。

爸爸试了那条库存，店员说："非常合适，有点儿长，但是别担心，只需要剪去一个大拇指的长度就好了。"

爸爸付了裤子的钱，然后回家了。到家后，他问妻子，"你可以在明天去野餐前帮我把裤子剪短一些吗？只需要剪短一个大拇指的长度就行了，我的确可以自己剪，但是每次我做针线活都会搞得一团糟。"

妈妈说："你没看见我有多忙吗？明天我们去野餐，首先我必须烘烤蛋糕，然后我还要切土豆和黄瓜用来做沙拉。"

"我能看到你有多忙。"爸爸叹了口气，说："我找尼娜帮忙。"

他发现大女儿正背着书包要出门，"尼娜，你能剪短我的裤子吗？明天要穿的，只需要剪短大拇指长度就行"。

"爸爸"，尼娜说，"看看妈妈给我的这个清单，首先

to the baker's and order fresh pita for tomorrow. Then I must buy drinks at the **grocery** store. Ask Max."

Max tugged at his father's sleeve. "Let me shorten them. I know what to do."

"Nonsense," said Papa, laughing. "You're too little."

Papa was disappointed he wouldn't be able to wear his new pants to the picnic. He went outside to water the garden.

Max lifted the pants off the hook. I'll show Papa that I'm not too young. After measuring the length of his thumb, Max cut a purple strip from each leg. Snip, snip. Then he folded the cut edges inside and stitched them with thread from Mama's **sewing** box. When Max hung the pants back on the hook in Papa's bedroom, he thought they looked as good as new.

When Nina came home from shopping, the pants were back on their hook. I hope Papa didn't think I was rude, rushing off like that. I can fix them now. Nina measured the length of her thumb. Snip, snip. When she finished hemming the pants, she returned them to Papa's room.

After everyone had gone to sleep, Mama put the last of the food in the

我必须去蛋糕单为明天的野餐订新鲜的披萨，然后我要去百货商店买饮料，你问问马克斯吧。"

马克斯拽了拽爸爸的袖子，"让我来吧，我知道怎么做。"

"瞎说，"爸爸笑着说，"你太小了。"

不能穿新裤子去野餐，爸爸感到失望。于是，他走到花园浇花。

马克斯把裤子从挂钩上取下来，我会向爸爸证明我并不小。量取大拇指长度，马克斯从每个裤腿剪下了一块紫色布料，咔嚓，咔嚓，然后他把剪好的裤边折进去，从妈妈的缝纫盒里拿出针线再把它们缝好。当把裤子放回爸爸房间的挂钩上时，他认为裤子看上去跟新的一样。

尼娜采购完回到家，裤子被放回了挂钩。我刚刚急匆匆地跑了，希望爸爸不会认为我不懂礼貌。我现在可以帮他做了。尼娜量取了拇指长度，咔嚓，咔嚓。完成裤子褶边后尼娜把裤子放回了爸爸房间。

大家都休息后，妈妈把最后一份食物放进冰箱，坐下来休息，她想起了可怜的爸

Papa's New Pants
爸爸的新裤子

refrigerator. She sat down to rest. Poor Papa, she thought. I'll fix those pants so he can wear them tomorrow. She **snipped** and stitched until the job was done.

When Papa woke up in the morning, he saw his new pants and sighed. Maybe no one will notice they're a bit too long, he thought. He pulled the pants on. What's going on here? He wondered. The family found him standing in front of the mirror.

Papa laughed so hard that tears rolled down his cheeks. When at last he could speak, he said, "Nobody wanted to disappoint me. What a great family I have!"

爸。我来搞定他的裤子，这样明天他就能穿上了。她剪短了裤子又缝缝补补直到裤子完全搞好。

爸爸早上醒来看见新裤子叹了口气，也许没人注意到我的裤子有点儿太长，他心里想。他穿上裤子。发生什么事情了？全家人发现他站在镜子前面。

爸爸笑得前俯后仰的直到眼泪都笑出来了，最后他终于能停下说话了，他说："所有人都不想让我失望，我有个一多么棒的家庭呀！"

单词解析 Word Analysis

shopkeeper [ˈʃɒpkiːpə(r)] *n.* 店主，老板

例 The advertised price was $168. The shopkeeper knocked off the odd shillings.
广告价格是168美元，但是店主减去了零头。

hem [hem] *v.* 缝……的褶边；给……镶边

例 Each dress is hemmed and scrupulously checked for imperfections.
每条连衣裙都缝上了褶边，并经过严格的检查，不允许有任何瑕疵。

satchel [ˈsætʃəl] *n.* 书包

例 He went off to school with a satchel over his shoulder.
他背着书包上学去了。

shorten ['ʃɔːtn] *v.* (使)变短，缩短
- 例 The trading day is shortened in observance of the Labor Day holiday.
  因庆祝劳动节，这个交易日交易时间缩短了。

grocery ['ɡrəʊsəri] *n.* 食品杂货店
- 例 He was employed at the local grocery store as a delivery boy.
  他受雇于当地杂货店当送货员。

sewing ['səʊɪŋ] *n.* 缝纫，缝补
- 例 We all got out our own sewing and sat in front of the log fire.
  我们都把自己的针线活拿出来，坐到了火堆前。

snip [snɪp] *v.* 剪下，剪断
- 例 He has now begun to snip away at the piece of paper.
  现在他已经开始剪这张纸。

语法知识点 Grammar Points

① **When Papa tried them on, the shopkeeper said, "A perfect fit. A little long, but don't worry."**

try on 试穿；恶作剧，本身on就是介词，所以一般后面加名词，名词也可以在中间。
- 例 I tried on a new coat yesterday, but it did not fit me well.
  我昨天试穿了一件外套，发现它根本不适合我。

② **Maybe no one will notice they're a bit too long, he thought. He pulled the pants on.**

a bit在肯定句中修饰动词、形容词、副词和比较级，表示"一点儿"的意思，too是副词，"太"的意思，是可以用a bit修饰的，翻译成"有点儿太……"
- 例 More such tools are coming, but it's a bit too early to disclose specific ones right now.
  未来会有更多这样的工具出现，但现在透露具体是哪款产品还为时过早。

pull on 穿上，戴上，相当于及物动词，以衣物做宾语，着重于穿戴的动作，多用于穿袜子、戴手套或是比较随便地穿上。

> She pulled on her coat and went out of the room hurriedly.
> 她穿上大衣，匆忙地走了。

③ Nobody wanted to disappoint me. What a great family I have!

感叹句是用来表示喜怒哀乐等强烈感情的句子。通常由how或what来引导。本句是由what引导的感叹句，what 是一个代词，故用来感叹名词，常用结构如下：

What+a/an+形容词+可数名词单数+主语+谓语

> What a beautiful girl she is!
> 她真是一个漂亮的姑娘！

What+形容词+不可数名词或可数名词复数+主语+谓语

> What cold weather it is!
> 天气好冷呀！

经典名句 Famous Classics

1. Honesty and diligence should be your eternal mates.
   诚实与勤勉应该成为你永久的伴侣。

2. Pay attention to your enemies, for they are the first to discover your mistakes.
   要重视你的敌人，因为是他们第一个发现你的错误。

3. Most folks are about as happy as they make up their minds to be.
   大多数人的快乐程度都是他们自己设定的。

4. Always bear in mind that your own resolution to succeed is more important than any other.
   永远记住，你成功的决心比什么都重要。

5. You can fool some of the people all of the time, and all of the people some of the time, but you cannot fool all of the people all of the time.
   你可以一直欺骗一些人，也可以在一定时间内欺骗所有人，但不可能一直欺骗所有人。

6. Children have more need of models than of critics.
儿童更需要的是榜样，而不是批评。

7. If you are not in good control of time or cannot set priorities for different matters, what you do is surely to be rebated.
不能充分掌握时间与区别事情的缓急先后，你做的一切都会打折扣。

8. There's nothing in the world so demoralizing as money.
世上没有任何东西比金钱更能使人道德败坏。

读书笔记